CHALLENGES TO DEMOCRACY

For information write to: Markus Wiener Publishers
114 Jefferson Road, Princeton, NJ 08540

Cover photo by Boris Kremer

Library of Congress Cataloging-in-Publication Data

Challenges to Democracy in the Middle East/Ahmad Ashraf . . . [et al.].
    Includes bibliographical references
    ISNB 1-55876-149-7
        1. Middle East—Politics and government—1979–.
    2. Democracy—Middle East.   3. Feminism—Turkey.
    I. Ashraf, Ahmad.
    DS63.7.C513   1997   96-48610
    956.05'3—dc21   CIP

Markus Wiener Publishers books are printed in the
United States of America on acid-free paper,
and meet the guidelines for permanence and durability
of the committee on production guidelines for book
longevity of the council on library resources.

Challenges to
Democracy
in the Middle East

William Harris
Amatzia Baram
Ahmad Ashraf
Heath Lowry
Yeşim Arat

Markus Wiener Publishers
Princeton

Contents

The Crisis of Democracy in Twentieth-Century Syria and Lebanon

WILLIAM HARRIS

Antecedents—Fragilities of Syria and Lebanon as new states

When Syria and Lebanon became independent states in the mid-1940s, both did so within the framework of parliamentary regimes established during French mandatory rule after 1920. Beirut and Damascus were major centers of Arab political innovation between the mid-nineteenth century and the Second World War, Albert Hourani's "Age of Arab Liberalism." The cosmopolitan society of Beirut served as a gateway for European influences and ideologies that stimulated reverberations in both Christian-dominated Mount Lebanon and the largely Sunni Muslim Syrian interior.

Initially, the bourgeois liberalism and nationalism of nineteenth-century Western Europe found echoes in the Levant in the mutually incompatible concepts of "Lebanonism" and "Arabism." "Lebanonism" involved the desire of Maronite Catholics for political separation from their mainly Muslim hinterland, and received concrete expression in the Greater Lebanon created by France in September 1920. "Arabism" started as a small movement among educated Christians and Muslims in late-nineteenth-century Beirut and Damascus, and aimed at Arab political independence from the Ottoman empire in the form of a single Arab state for the Ottoman Arab provinces.

1

After the British defeated the Ottomans in 1917, "Arabism" immediately became the leading political concept in the Levant, boosted both by the brief existence of Feisal's "Arab kingdom" based in Damascus and by Arab hostility to the Franco-British political takeover of the region. Modern Syria, comprising what remained of geographical Syria after the creation of Greater Lebanon and the British mandate of Palestine, meant nothing to its population and seethed with discontent through a quarter-century of French domination. Strident Arab nationalism set the parameters for political competition in interior Syria, whereas "Arabism" faced an uphill struggle against "Lebanonism" and sectarian agendas in Greater Lebanon. This situation between 1920 and 1945 set the scene for unhappy later dénouements: dictatorship in Damascus and violent fragmentation in Beirut.

"Arabism" and militant socialist and fascist tendencies—which like Arab nationalism were derived from contemporary European models—converged in Syria under the French mandatory regime. Elaboration of European-style administrative and economic infrastructure, together with extension of primary and secondary education, had significant political implications. A new petite bourgeoisie emerged to challenge the commercial and landholding elite, while the French stimulated a political awakening among the peasants and heterodox Islamic-derived communities of the rural peripheries—most notably the 'Alawis of the Mediterranean coastal mountains and the Druze of the Jabal al-Duruz, south of Damascus. In the 1930s Communism and the "Greater Syria" of Antun Sa'ada's Syrian Social Nationalist Party made inroads among urban youth and intellectuals, and the upper-class politicians sought to hold their followings by founding fascist-style youth movements, such as the Steelshirts and the National League. This provided the background for the emergence in the late 1940s of the pan-Arabist Ba'th Party, which melded romantic secular nationalism with social radicalism and called for revolutionary struggle to overthrow the high bourgeoisie and mold a "new Arab man."

The French deliberately pursued political fragmentation as a cheap means of controlling a hostile population. They tried to separate 'Alawis and Druze from the Sunni majority; they manipulated and humiliated the moderate nationalist factions of the urban elite; and they created a local armed force with a small indigenous officer corps that offered social advancement for members of the petite bourgeoisie and the religious minorities. At the same time, French determination to shackle Syria to the weak French currency and economy, combined with the hardship of the Great Depression, restricted economic opportunities and intensified popular bitterness.

The experiences of Feisal's brief assertion of Arab independence in 1919–20 and the Great Revolt of 1926–27, when a Druze insurrection coalesced with a nationalist uprising in Damascus, made it very difficult for Syria's high bourgeois nationalist leaders to balance between the French and the "street." Compromise with France was necessary to extract greater political autonomy and to safeguard elite social interests, but French maneuvering and refusal to honor commitments under the 1936 Franco-Syrian treaty discredited bourgeois politicians.

After independence in 1945 Syria's ruling class was weak and divided, with no coherent vision beyond the preservation of its privileges. Loyalty to the new country within its established boundaries was virtually nonexistent, the elite had no serious command of social forces, and the government marginalized Syria's new army, whose officer corps generally did not derive from the upper bourgeoisie. Sunni army commanders turned against the Sunni politicians after the 1949 defeat by Israel, and Syria looked ahead to political ferment.

In contrast, Greater Lebanon came out of the period of the French mandate with a more stable, united elite that had a firmer grip on politics and society. First, unlike interior Syria, Lebanon had a background of practice with political autonomy and semi-parliamentary institutions through the half-century of experimentation with the *mutasarrifiyya* (autonomous province) of Mount Lebanon after 1860. Second, whereas in Syria the French aimed to splinter and subjugate the population, in Lebanon France sought to ensure the viability of the enlarged entity by encouraging sectarian pluralism and collaboration between the Christian and Muslim elites. In the 1930s Sunni and Shi'i leaders slowly became reconciled to Greater Lebanon, Maronite leaders began to tire of French paternalism, and a solid basis emerged for the 1943 Maronite-Sunni National Pact, which gave independent Lebanon a more-or-less coherent ruling class.

Overall, the compartmentalization of Lebanon as a jumble of sectarian minorities retarded the development of ideological and issue-based parties and helped the high bourgeoisie to dominate the population through patronage networks. In Syria social conditions were much more conducive to ideological mobilization: the overwhelming majority of Syrians were convulsed by Arab nationalism, about 70% of the population were Sunni Muslims, and political activists among the largest single minority—the 'Alawis—were more interested in social revolution than in sectarian assertion.

In contrast, Lebanon's confessional democracy was little more than a game of musical chairs for a limited circle of upper class families, with disproportionate roles for Maronites and Sunnis. The most vociferous challenges to the presidencies of Bishara al-Khuri (1943–52) and Camille Chamoun (1952–58) came from within the elite, unlike the more dramatic ideological crosscurrents that were tearing Syria apart in the 1950s. Nonetheless, the contradictions between Maronite and Muslim visions—Western-oriented "Lebanonism" versus Arab nationalism—were enough to bring a temporary collapse of the political system in 1958.

Beirut's real superiority to Damascus from the mid-nineteenth century onward involved its openness to the world beyond the eastern Mediterranean and the development of the most sophisticated Arab civil society. In the realms of publishing, private education, proliferation of a free press, independent professional organizations, and general public freedoms, Beirut towered above the rest of the Arab world by the 1960s. A flourishing civil society provided social networks and arenas for public debate that could eventually have supported a genuine representative and participatory democracy.

In the critical decades of the mid-twentieth century, however, the Lebanese elite failed the tests of political and social responsibility. Instead of giving the urban poor and the awakening Shi'i masses a decent stake in a pluralist Lebanon, the ruling class adhered rigidly to the unfettered liberal capitalism of the "merchant republic." Beirut's encircling "belt of misery" was ignored and Maronite bosses were determined to maintain the existing political system regardless of demographic shifts in favor of Muslims in general and Shi'is in particular. By the 1960s Arab nationalism was in decline, the brief Egyptian-Syrian union had collapsed, and the various communities of Greater Lebanon had evolved a common sense of Lebanese identity. A more accommodatory strategy from the elite at this stage could have supplied Lebanon with the cohesion it needed to cope with the Arab-Israeli stresses of the late 1960s and early 1970s. Unfortunately, after 1970 Lebanon had a disastrously incompetent president—Sulayman Faranjiyya—whose erratic political behavior and primitive "free market" proclivities sealed the country's fate. Faranjiyya, who was quite oblivious to the consequences of his behavior and policies, illustrates the decisive role an individual personality can play at a critical historical moment.

In the 1950s Syria undoubtedly lacked the social framework to sustain its parliamentary regime. The local press had no serious standing, and the scattering of unions and professional organizations was vulnerable to takeover by radical political movements. Although the faltering hold of Syria's upper-class factions meant that Syria temporarily boasted a more interesting political landscape than Lebanon, a number of features ensured that the period of competing agendas did not last long. Syria's status as the main arena of pan-Arab competition in the 1950s, chiefly between Egypt and Iraq, eliminated any chance of stable parliamentary government and truncated the development of civil society. Further, regular military interventions after 1949 prevented any entrenchment of pluralist politics.

Most ominously, the new political forces seeking to transform Syrian society were without exception absolutist and intolerant of alternative viewpoints. Ba'thists, Communists, Syrian Social Nationalists, Nasirites, and the Muslim Brotherhood all dreamed of seizing power, imposing their programs, and purging their rivals. For a few years in the 1950s they sparred with one another and with the elite factions, mobilizing the peasantry and the urban "street." In the end, however, one of the parties was bound to triumph and to forge an autocratic *sulta* (authority) of the type well known in Middle Eastern history, regardless of ideology or class origins.

Syria's disorderly, incomplete pluralism had its high tide with the 1954 parliamentary elections,[1] perhaps the most interesting ever held in the Arab world and as free as any in contemporary Lebanon. The Ba'th, linking with Akram Hawrani's peasant following in Sunni central Syria, made a strong showing, but independents and loose groupings still took a majority of seats, a sign that the Syrian people were only just beginning to get used to issue-based politics. The elections marked a decisive setback for the bid by Iraq's monarchical regime to subordinate Syria, and aroused concern in London and Washington about gains for militant anti-Western elements. Indeed, the few relatively free democratic experiments in the modern Arab world have generally caused more nervousness than enthusiasm in the West.

After 1954 Syria became destabilized and radicalized by external interference, as a focus of strategic confrontation both among Arab regimes and between the U.S. and the Soviet Union. Parliamentarianism wilted, the country itself seemed irrelevant in the atmosphere of populist Arabism, and in 1958 the Ba'th and other Arab nationalists put Syria under the command of Gamal 'Abd al-Nasir in the United Arab Republic (U.A.R.). The Syrians could only tolerate Egyptian domination for three years, but the U.A.R. dealt a mortal blow to political pluralism, opening the way to decades of Ba'thist dictatorship.

Politics and power in Asad's Syria

In the 1960s Syria underwent a revolutionary transformation. Army officers, principally 'Alawis, took over the Ba'th—the country's most dynamic political movement—after the party's civilian leaders had been tarnished by their association with the failed U.A.R. The military wing of the Ba'th achieved power by stages after the party seized the central role in the Syrian government in a March 1963 coup; Ba'thist officers skilfully undermined party opponents and non-Ba'thist army commanders, concluding the process with their own coup in February 1966. In broad terms, this marked a political displacement of urban, Sunni Syria by the historically oppressed rural peripheries and sectarian minorities. A small group of 'Alawis rose through the Ba'th and the armed forces to rule Syria. The Ba'th attracted them by its secularism, Arabism, and semi-socialism; the armed forces were scorned by most of the Sunni bourgeoisie, and thus open to penetration by non-Sunnis.

In the mid- to late 1960s the Ba'thist regime of Salah Jadid, an 'Alawi officer who operated under a figurehead Sunni president, Nur al-Din al-Atasi, dispossessed much of the urban and rural bourgeoisie, nationalizing industries and banks and redistributing landholdings. It also asserted militant nationalism against Israel and "Arab reaction." By 1970 these policies threatened Syria's viability. In November of that year Defense Minister Hafiz al-Asad removed Jadid and al-Atasi, and in February 1971 made himself Syria's first 'Alawi president. Asad moderated regime economic policies, to give a little more room for private enterprise and the black market, and pursued a highly pragmatic external policy—but there was no political liberalization. Asad's purpose was to entrench authoritarianism.

Through the 1970s, when subsidies from the Gulf oil sheikhdoms and economic expansion marginally tempered the rigor of the regime, vestiges of the open politics of the 1950s could still be detected. Official candidates were defeated in 1972 elections for provincial administrations;[2] the Syrian Bar Association launched a Committee for Human Rights in 1977 and made frequent protests between 1977 and 1980;[3] and October 1978 union elections saw gains for Communists, Nasirites, Islamists, and independents. All this was abruptly terminated in 1980–81, as part of the crackdown against the Muslim Brotherhood.

Three processes in Asad's Syria, all of which intensified during the 1980s, made future democratization unlikely. First, Asad consolidated a secret police state that made a mockery of constitutional norms and formal institutions. The official government structure—prime minister, cabinet, parliament, and bureaucracy—bore no relationship to the realities of power and became merely a façade for control of Syria by a coterie of intelligence agency bosses, military men, and relatives and confidants of the president (categories that obviously overlapped). The 1971 "Progressive National Front" of the Ba'th, the Communist Party, and assorted Nasirites—later grotesquely billed by Asad as Syria's advance version of Eastern European liberalization[4]—entrapped and emasculated the regime's political competitors. Even the Ba'th party became simply a mechanism for vote mobilization and propaganda. Human rights and judicial autonomy, enshrined in writing in the 1973 constitution, were routinely flouted under "emergency" rule. Nobody in Syria believed that the appearance of anything coincided with its reality, with the exception of the readiness to resort to brute force. Patrick Seale writes of Asad's image of himself as a "man of institutions,"[5] but in fact the Syrian president systematically destroyed the credibility of public institutions. This meant that Ba'thist Syria had no basis left for political liberalization.

Second, the regime used the media, the education system, and intelligence service surveillance of the population to enforce absolute ideological uniformity. For the Ba'th anyone who favored serious political pluralism, who commented about sectarian distinctions, or who dissented from the ideas and policies of "our leader for ever," could only be an "enemy of the Arabs" or a "proto-Zionist" (*mutasahayun*). By the 1980s the regime considered such people legitimate targets for arrest, torture, and even murder. The population became habituated to a "political culture" of fear, in which self-censorship was a major feature of everyday conversation and individuals were encouraged to inform on one another. Schools, newspapers, television, and radio pursued a relentless campaign of brainwashing, particularly targeting the younger generation. From watching Syrian television in the mid-1980s I recall advertisements depicting Asad's face beaming down on Damascus from within the rising sun. An Armenian friend from Beirut who had visited family in Aleppo had tales of the indoctrination of young relatives in Ba'thist youth organizations and children being instructed to report parental political discussions. Such psychological conditioning, added to the hatred created by prolonged repression, militated against political tolerance and democratic values—regardless of the outside world's intrusion through new communications technology in the 1990s.

Third, subversion of Syria's embryonic civil society began with the corporatization of trade unions and the temporary abolition of political parties under the U.A.R. From 1958 on, with a brief hiatus in the early 1960s, Syrian governments subjected autonomous organizations—trade unions, professional associations, private education, sports and cultural clubs—to steerage by the state and the Ba'th party. Determined pulverization of civil society, however, began only in the late 1970s, when Asad felt threatened by opposition elements, most prominently the Muslim Brotherhood. In 1980 the regime deployed armed agents to purge "enemies of the people"—Communists, Islamists, and Nasirites—from trade unions, the Peasant Union, and the teachers' organization.[6] In 1980–81 the

Syrian Bar Association, the Human Rights Committee, and all other professional groups were dismantled, with the professional associations reappearing as extensions of the Ba'th.[7] Through the following fifteen years civil society effectively ceased to exist, with only a few twitchings of dissent beneath the suffocating bulk of the regime. This state of affairs persists into the late 1990s, almost a decade after its demise in the old Eastern Bloc. It is difficult to imagine an easy reintroduction of democratic debate or civic responsibility on such barren terrain.

Between 1976 and 1982 the Syrian dictatorship faced a crisis that has shaped its outlook and policies ever since. In those years Ba'thist absolutism was challenged by the Islamist absolutism of the Muslim Brotherhood, and the regime nearly foundered. The Syrian Brotherhood, an offshoot of the original movement established by Hasan al-Banna in Egypt in 1928, was only a minor political tendency among Syria's Sunni Muslim majority in the 1950s and 60s. However, it expanded rapidly in the main towns of northern and central Syria in the 1970s, in reaction to Ba'thist secularism and 'Alawi command of the state—even as Asad extended the Ba'th's patronage networks among Sunnis. The Brotherhood linked with other opposition parties to protest Syria's 1976 intervention against the Palestinians in Lebanon and asserted its adherence to democratic principles. However, there was no doubt that the Brotherhood aspired to establish its own version of an "Islamic state" in which the 30% of Syrians who belonged to sectarian minorities would be relegated to permanent second-class status or worse. It spearheaded a campaign of assassinations against Ba'thists, and gave 'Alawis good reason to fear for their existence.

The regime responded with the utmost ferocity. After gunmen killed eighty-three 'Alawi military cadets in Aleppo in June 1979, the government declared membership of the Brotherhood a capital offense, the security forces rounded up thousands of suspects, and street disturbances and strikes in Aleppo and Hama were answered with ruthless suppression. The Brotherhood received assistance from anti-Syrian elements in Lebanon, including the Maronite militia, and from Iraq, both of which infuriated Asad, but the rebellion was doomed by the fragmentation of the Syrian opposition and its failure to stir Damascus, where the regime had made particular efforts to broaden its urban support. Asad finally smashed the Brotherhood in a spectacular dénouement in Hama in February 1982. The full weight of the Syrian army, including artillery, air power, and chemical weapons, was brought to bear against a local uprising; the old city of Hama was levelled and up to 20,000 people killed in two weeks of bombardments and massacres. Thereafter the Brotherhood shrank to a few bands of exiles, some of whom sought reconciliation with the regime in the 1990s.

On the one hand, Ba'thist Syria became the first and only Middle Eastern state effectively to wipeout political Islamism on its territory—ironically, in view of Syria's subsequent role as an ally of Lebanese and Palestinian Islamist groups. On the other hand, even as conformity settled over the country, the regime knew that Sunni Syria was psychologically scarred and that Hama would never be forgotten. Asad and the ruling clique could not afford to relax either their grip or their vigilance. In the 1990s economic liberalization was thus conceived as a means of avoiding political liberalization. Further, the Brotherhood bid for an "Islamic state" brought an unprecedented coalescence of 'Alawis and Christians—the two leading minorities—and set up potential lines of sectarian confrontation in the case of an Islamist resurgence: a long-term scenario of chaos, not democracy.

I visited Hama in March 1983, a year after the insurrection. I walked through the ruins of the old city, where piles of rubble had been bulldozed onto the Orontes river banks, and climbed the citadel hill for a panorama of the devastation. It was a depressing, cloudy, gray day and the scene bore more than a passing resemblance to images of Hiroshima after the atomic bomb blast—several huge "holes" ripped out of the urban landscape. The great mosque, one of the finest in the Middle East, no longer existed. It was Friday midday, but no call to prayer could be heard. Two air force fighters circled high above the mutilated remains of the town center. I thought of the land of Mordor in Tolkien's *Lord of the Rings*.

Later I spoke with a local resident who had a small second-floor hostel—the hotels listed in guidebooks were either flattened or closed. He pulled me back from his balcony because "the *mukhabarat* 'intelligence agents¡ might notice you." Outside it was unnaturally quiet for an Arab city; people shuffled about like zombies. Hama was surreal.

Through the mid-1980s Syria had to cope with grave economic difficulties, arising from isolation in the Arab and international arenas, declining oil prices, and the non-competitiveness of the Eastern European-style public sector. Consequences included near-bankruptcy of the Syrian state, sliding real incomes for most Syrians, inability to sustain the objective of strategic parity with Israel, and weakness in Lebanon. In the late 1980s the disintegration of the Soviet Union removed Syria's superpower patron and left Asad even more exposed. To salvage the situation, the Syrian regime relaxed its tight economic controls from 1986 on, giving private businesses opportunities unprecedented under Ba'thism to amass foreign currency, buy lands, and generally make profits without state intervention.

Saddam Husayn's seizure of Kuwait in August 1990 decisively helped Asad, as Syria transformed its international situation by joining the U.S.-led coalition against Iraq. Damascus received an American "green light" to take control of Lebanon, and thereafter to move toward an integration of the two countries that would be highly profitable for the Syrians. More immediately Damascus absorbed about $3 billion of payoffs for participation in the coalition from the Gulf oil states, Germany, and Japan. In May 1991 Investment Law No. 10 completed the transition to an economy in which the public sector depended on private sector investments and export earnings to ensure the viability of the whole Ba'thist apparatus. This law included new tax breaks, tariff concessions, and currency conversion provisions that accelerated the emergence of a new commercial high bourgeoisie, and buttressed the turnaround toward growth in the Syrian economy.

Hafiz al-Asad conceived the economic liberalization (*infitah*) of the late 1980s and early 1990s as a Chinese-style exercise to gain resources and domestic allies for the indefinite perpetuation of authoritarianism. He rejected any parallel with the events of the early 1990s in Eastern Europe, where the collapse of centrally planned economies went hand in hand with political transformation. The Syrian regime made some pragmatic adjustments to accommodate changes in the balance of economic and social interests, but these should not for a moment be interpreted as real political liberalization.

More independents gained seats in the 1990 parliamentary elections, mainly businessmen and professionals, and up to 5,000 Islamist political prisoners were released in stages.[8] First, the ruling 'Alawi-Ba'thist-military combine sought a more solid alliance with the private sector, and to give this sector a stake in the political status quo. Syria was becoming even more obviously a state in which the Western distinction between "legality" and "criminality" had little meaning, and in which the veneer of Ba'thist austerity was completely at variance with the drive of the ruling class to amass private wealth by any means. Second, with Islamism neutered inside Syria and in view of the regime's alignments with Islamists outside Syria, it made good sense to have a stage-managed rapprochement with people whose political lives were finished, and to exhibit sensitivity to the increased public piety of urban Sunnis in the 1990s—as long as such piety had no political dimension. By 1996 the remnants of the Muslim Brotherhood were reduced to apologizing for past behavior, claiming that military action had never been their "original choice."[9]

Away from the modus vivendi with business interests, the regime remained rigidly intolerant toward dissent. For example, a small human rights group surfaced in 1989, encouraged by events in Eastern Europe and Syria's more freewheeling commercial orientation. It did not last long. It criticized the 99.9% "yes" vote in favor of Asad in the November 1991 presidential referendum,[10] and was promptly broken up. As Islamists came out of the prisons, human rights activists went in, a nasty case of "revolving doors." Volker Perthes notes the undiminished degradation of civil society; in the early 1990s the number of authorized private associations was actually lower than in the aftermath of the crackdown in the early 1980s.[11]

As for Islamists, the Syrian regime could abandon its relaxed stance in an instant when required. In the mid-1990s Syria hosted an assortment of "Afghan Arabs," Islamist radicals who had fought against the Russians in Afghanistan and who then turned against pro-Western Arab governments. Some were wanted by Egypt for subversion, and others used Syria as a base for infiltration into Jordan, obviously with the knowledge and approval of Damascus. However, American fury after the deadly June 1996 bomb attack against U.S. military personnel in Saudi Arabia suddenly made "Afghan Arabs" a liability. The Syrians lost no time in herding them into detention.[12]

Most significantly, economic liberalization and a growth rate of about 7% per annum in the early 1990s could not resolve underlying contradictions in Syrian society or relieve the basic predicament of Ba'thist Syria. Benefits of growth went almost entirely to private capitalists and the upper echelon of the regime, with the great majority of the Syrian people dependent on stagnant wages and salaries, and facing falling living standards. In other words, for most Syrians the 1990s were not much different from the 1980s. An inefficient, overstaffed bureaucracy and a vast, hopelessly uncompetitive array of public enterprises—Syria's "Eastern Bloc" face—continued to overshadow the private sector. Perpetuation of this situation made it unlikely that private sector florescence would ever do anything but enrich part of the bourgeoisie, providing no benefit at all to most Syrians.

At the same time Syria's population continued to increase at 3–4% per annum, among the highest demographic growth rates in the world. Despite a decline after the mid-1980s, this growth rate promised that a population of about 14 million in 1996 would inflate to over 25 million before 2010. There was no hope that the Ba'thist apparatus and the private sector could absorb more than a minority of new entrants to the labor force, which meant the ranks of discontented, poor, underemployed Syrians would steadily expand. In 1993–95, between 500,000 and one million Syrian workers (perhaps one-quarter of working-age male Syrians) streamed across the border into Lebanon to provide cheap labor for that country's "reconstruction"[13]—a sign that the Syrian economy was fundamentally defective. After all, Lebanon in the mid-1990s was itself a devastated, ramshackle society where the average wage barely sufficed to buy essential groceries.

In the last years of the twentieth century the Syrian dictatorship needed to maintain its old support base in the salaried lower middle class, the peasantry, and the public sector while its top personnel migrated into new alignments with commercial capitalists. It also had to keep itself afloat on the rising demographic tide, to prepare for a transition to a new leadership, and to cope with new twists in the evolution of Arab-Israeli affairs. The leadership issue was not simply a matter of the regime's dependence on management by one man—Hafiz al-Asad—who was 67 in 1997, in poor health, and with no visible successor. It related more generally to the aging of Asad's team at the summit of the regime. Syria's situation in the late 1990s seemed to require flexible thinking to generate imaginative solutions—in short, wider political debate. However, the Ba'thist state had deliberately destroyed whatever framework for pluralism had existed in Syria, and the regime could only be expected to respond to domestic dilemmas and regional uncertainty with tried and trusted methods.

Political sterility, public avoidance of controversy, and the general drabness of life encouraged mass escapism into fantasy worlds. Through the summer of 1996 a romantic Mexican television soap opera, "Cassandra," captivated Syrians.[14] The series dominated public discourse, became a reference point for social timetables and meetings, and stimulated popular jokes. Merchants and shopkeepers labelled everything from dresses and perfumes to watermelons and sweets "Cassandra," the name of the heroine of the series. A bride at a village wedding in central Syria refused to have the ceremony until after the evening episode; another bride elsewhere delayed the wedding contract on the same basis, and the celebration then became funereal, with tears and weeping, because one of the series' heroes had died. I saw the same soap opera in Beirut the preceding summer; it was popular but certainly did not produce the mass obsession evident in Syria. Even after six years of an increasingly oppressive new Lebanese order, the Lebanese people still had wider horizons and more diversions than the Syrians.

The bitter fruits of Lebanon's war

Lebanon's war period, from 1975 to 1990, destroyed the confessional democracy of 1943–75. The elite that managed the system changed substantially in character and composition; much of the middle class that had operated Lebanon's civil society either fled overseas or was pauperized by currency depreciation; and the Christian and Muslim population lost its earlier respect for *zucama* (political bosses) and patronage networks. The population resented more and more bitterly the humiliations of *wasta* (the need for a patron to intercede for almost any bureaucratic service). The legitimacy of high bourgeois confessional democracy among the Lebanese people depended on a minimum of respect for the political leadership and a minimum of consent for the electoral manipulation and factional maneuvering that sustained the ruling oligarchy—all of which eroded during the war period.

The management of Lebanese society by the multisectarian high bourgeoisie was decisively disrupted by prolonged sectarian compartmentalization of the population in the 1970s and 80s, by the takeover of most of the country by militias or non-Lebanese forces during those years, and by the reformulation of the elite itself. In the 1970s two charismatic "outsiders," Musa Sadr and Bashir Jumayyil, mobilized Shi'is and Maronites. Unfortunately, both were pre-eminently sectarian leaders who embodied the demands and fears of their respective communities and who assisted the dissolution of the country into de facto cantons.

Musa Sadr founded the Shi'i Amal movement in 1975; Amal was the first organization to express the political frustration of Lebanon's largest community vis-à-vis command of confessional democracy by Maronite and Sunni *zucama*. In 1978, Bashir Jumayyil established Lebanon's largest sectarian militia—the mainly Maronite Lebanese Forces—and organized a powerful, virtually autonomous Christian sector centered in East Beirut. Musa Sadr vanished on a visit to Libya in 1978 and Bashir Jumayyil was killed by a car bomb in 1982. After they had gone, warlords and war profiteers continued to flourish, operating in a patchwork of militia fiefdoms and zones controlled by foreign armies. Despite the inglorious Israeli incursion as far as Beirut in 1982–83, the most extensive, enduring external overlordship was that of the Syrians, who came in 1976 to save the Maronites from the Palestinians and the Lebanese leftist forces of Druze chief Kamal Junblatt. Thereafter Syria always controlled at least half the country.

Through the war period a host of militia leaders, nouveaux riches, and Syrian favorites jostled with the older elite families for command of Lebanese society, producing a new upper class that would have to impose itself by force in any reconstructed Lebanese state. There was no chance that such an unsavory hodgepodge could replicate the circumstances of 1943–75, for most of which time the high bourgeoisie who had established the 1943 National Pact ruled with the voluntary approval of the majority of Lebanese. One important reason for the new state of affairs after the mid-1980s was the lack of a social buffer between the reformulated elite and the impoverished "street" of both Christians and Muslims—wartime conditions had devastated the middle class underpinnings of confessional democracy. Confessional democracy needed a large, cooperative middle class for its staffing and legitimization. By 1990 much of this portion of Lebanon's people was living abroad, and not likely to return under the sort of regime that afflicted the country after 1990.

The populism mobilized by Musa Sadr and Bashir Jumayyil acquired new dimensions in the mid-1980s: the Islamism of Hizballah (the Party of God) for poorer Shi'is, and rejection of militias in all communities, but particularly in the Christian sector. In the late 1980s discontent with militias crystallized into the romantic, secular nationalism promoted by General Michel Aoun, commander of the Lebanese army.

Hizballah and Aounism had some common features. They both gained much popular momentum from the collapse of Lebanon's economy and currency in the mid-1980s, which irretrievably discredited militia cantons. They were both incompatible with existing power structures in Lebanon's principal communities: Hizballah threatened Amal's position among Shi'is, and Michel Aoun challenged the Lebanese Forces militia and the old elite in the Christian sector. Above all, they both opposed the status quo in the eastern Mediterranean. Hizballah, backed by the Islamic revolutionary regime in Iran, aspired to an "Islamic state" in Lebanon, attacked the U.S., kidnapped Westerners, and fought the Israelis, whose 1982 occupation of southern Lebanon had brought the party into existence. Aoun sought to overthrow the militia cantons and chase Syria out of Lebanon. In the end, of course, their agendas differed radically, and Hizballah and Aoun fought different enemies; they were in the same small country, but inhabited separate universes.

Nonetheless, when Lebanon's parliament (in its fifth self-extended term since the 1972 elections) failed to select a new president in September 1988, with Aoun then forming a provisional military government in East Beirut and launching a "war of liberation" against Syria in March 1989, the U.S. placed him in the same category as Hizballah as a threat to "regional stability." The U.S. wanted to take advantage of the end of the Cold War to settle the Lebanese and Arab-Israeli crises, in order to stabilize the hinterland of the Gulf oil reservoir. The preferred cheap solution for Lebanon was to put it under Syrian guardianship; the U.S. hoped that Syria would thereafter make a deal with Israel and clamp down on Lebanese Islamists.

In October 1989 the U.S. coordinated with Syria to resurrect high bourgeois management of Lebanon, by a constitutional agreement extracted from Lebanese parliamentarians in the Saudi city of Ta'if. The Ta'if agreement equalized Christian and MuslimвDruze representation in parliament and the cabinet, with the balance of authority shifting from the Maronite Christian president to the Sunni Muslim prime minister and the Shi'i Muslim parliamentary speaker. In reality these matters had little relevance to the wider population, which was to see virtually nothing of either representation or participation, and the Ta'if agreement's political allocations were overshadowed by Syrian guidance of the new Lebanese regime.

Vicious fighting in 1989–90 in both the Shi'i and Christian arenas softened up the Lebanese population for imposition of Syrian overlordship. Hizballah fought Amal to a standstill in Beirut's southern suburbs and southern Lebanon, and in East Beirut, where a defiant Michel Aoun blocked implementation of the Ta'if agreement, U.S. and Syrian interference[15] contributed to a terrible showdown between Aoun's army brigades and the Lebanese Forces militia in February–May 1990. Leading Shi'i *calim* (religious scholar) Muhammad Husayn Fadlallah, carefully avoiding any mention of Syria, observed that "it was necessary, from the American standpoint, to fragment the Christian people, as the Islamic people had already been fragmented, because America wishes a shattering of Lebanon's balances . . . And this can only be via a shattering of the two great Lebanese sects, the Shi'is and the Maronites."[16] In October 1990, as a reward for cooperating with the U.S. against Iraq, the U.S. allowed Syria to expel a weakened Aoun from the Ba'abda presidential palace.

From late 1990 on, a symbiotic relationship evolved between Lebanon's Ta'if regime and its Syrian patron, a relationship unique in the post–Cold War world. Nowhere else does a government that claims to be sovereign seek the approval of a neighboring state for every aspect of its domestic policies, even including bureaucratic appointments. Nowhere else are parliamentary and presidential elections so blatantly supervised by a foreign power. The U.S. has facilitated the creation and perpetuation of these circumstances as an integral dimension of its Middle Eastern policies. Yet the U.S. repeatedly asserts that it backs "independence" and "democracy" for Lebanon. In light of the evidence, such assertions are simply deceitful.

In the 1990s the Lebanese and Syrian ruling classes developed important joint characteristics and interests. Despite the survival in Lebanon of *zucama* and old high bourgeois elements whose counterparts in Syria were displaced by the Ba'th in the 1960s, the differences in elite social backgrounds diminished after the 1975 collapse of "National Pact" Lebanon. In Lebanon, the rise of lower-middle-class personnel via the militias, the wartime "informal" economy, and diaspora opportunities meant that by the 1990s a major segment of the Lebanese elite had similar social origins to the Syrian Ba'thists. In Syria, economic liberalization after the mid-1980s gave the Syrian elite a private business flavor more compatible with the freewheeling commercial orientation of the Lebanese.

As for common interests, Syria needed willing staff for a credible proxy regime that would promote the strategic integration of the two countries and organize Lebanon's economy in a manner conducive to Syrian financial siphonings. Lebanon's business moguls needed security guarantees to protect them from the hostility of the Lebanese people as they converted Lebanon into something resembling a private plantation (*mazraca*). The implementation of these agendas meant that Lebanon's new constitution and governing institutions became little more than a Syrian-style façade, which had little to do with the realities of power or decision making.

After some hesitation, Damascus opted in October 1992 for the Lebanese Saudi billionaire Rafiq al-Hariri as the most suitable front man for Lebanon's new order. Hariri had an ambitious "reconstruction" project and an impressive network of connections in the Gulf and Europe for mobilizing loans and investment; he seemed the person most likely to create profitable pastures for Syria and the Lebanese elite. After 1992 all three of the Lebanese regime's leading personalities were from the ranks of the nouveaux riches. Sunni Prime Minister Hariri was a self-made man, an outsider in relation to Lebanon's leading Sunni families.

Maronite President Ilyas al-Hirawi came from a middle-class background in Zahla, where the Greek Catholic Skaffs headed the local social hierarchy. Shi'i Parliamentary Speaker Nabih Barri epitomized the new generation of Shi'i politicians brought into prominence by Musa Sadr; he had made money in the diaspora and rose to command the Amal militia in the 1980s. They all interacted comfortably with Syrian officials, were easily overawed by Asad, and lacked the bothersome prestige of Lebanon's great political families.

Hariri's foreign connections deterred the Syrians a little, until they concluded that these could be made useful—after all, his construction company had helped build Syria's new presidential palace, a huge black edifice on the Mazza hill above Damascus that epitomized Asad's autocracy. After 1992, cabinet posts and senior bureaucratic positions were almost all reserved either for Hariri's business and professional colleagues or for Syria's allies and clients. In late 1996 Hariri entered parliament at the head of a bloc of more than 30 personal associates, in elections the results of which were predetermined by the regime and the Syrians.

Nobody in authority in Lebanon's "second republic" had the slightest sympathy with western-style democratic procedures, and the major single priority in state spending involved inflating the army to more than double its 1975 size.[17] The plain purpose was to repress the population while a small minority took advantage of the new horizons for profiteering opened up by "reconstruction," real estate speculation, and allocation of funds from massively expanded public debt. President Hirawi stated flatly that "security comes before bread,"[18] and the Interior Minister indicated that the government had "Syrian backing"[19] in case the Lebanese army proved inadequate. At most, perhaps one-fifth of Lebanon's people found ways to improve their circumstances, whether grandly or modestly—a portion of these sufficed to fill the cafes and night-clubs, impressing some Western journalists. The rest, like their counterparts in Yeltsin's Russia and other such places, faced only a grim struggle for survival in the "new order."

Under Hariri and Hirawi, Lebanon experienced a steady slide into the sterile authoritarianism that characterizes much of the Arab world. This had two main dimensions: the de facto confederation with Syria, and the regime's determination to erode Lebanon's civil society. The May 1991 Treaty of Brotherhood, Cooperation, and Coordination, itself an expression of the call in the Ta'if Agreement for detailed pacts between Syria and Lebanon, outlined institutional arrangements for linking the two countries, principally a "High Council" with a permanent secretariat. The treaty served as an umbrella for a succession of accords concerning military, economic, and social affairs. The August 1991 Defense and Security Pact, for example, connected Lebanon's security organizations with the Syrian apparatus, and demanded "the banning of any activity . . . in all military, security, political, and information fields that might endanger and cause threats to the other country"[20]—a requirement technically incompatible with free elections in Lebanon. Syria openly dictated the evolution of Lebanese politics; in October 1996 Hafiz al-Asad intervened personally to have the Lebanese parliament extend Hirawi's presidential term.

Partnership with a dictatorship that set all the parameters for the relationship could hardly be termed conducive to democratic procedures. In 1996 Lebanon's fate provided a warning for Hong Kong's future with the People's Republic of China—Syria's "model" in the 1990s—with the crucial distinction that the international community continued to regard Lebanon as a sovereign state, not as a province of Syria.

Given that many of the hundreds of thousands of Syrians working in Lebanon in the mid-1990s functioned as informants for Syrian military intelligence, Lebanese had to be careful about casual public conversations. In July 1995 I had an interesting encounter in a service taxi in West Beirut. I was speaking in English with my son in the back seat, and listening to the driver lecturing a Shi'i Lebanese passenger about "We Shi'is . . ." The Lebanese man said little beyond a few guarded platitudes. After he left, the driver turned to me and said: *Inta mu lubnaani* (You are not Lebanese . . .). He then asked a series of questions about what I was doing in Beirut. The use of the Syrian form of "not," together with his previous discourse, gave him away as a Syrian 'Alawi. I refrained from responding: *Inta mu lubnaani kamaan* (You also are not Lebanese), and asking if he had work other than taxi-driving.

As regards Lebanon's civil society, which remained the most vibrant in the Arab world even after Lebanon's war period, Hariri's government plainly favored control and corporatization, thus bringing Beirut more into line with Damascus. Syria's intimidatory military and secret police presence within Lebanon already meant that the trend toward integration between the two countries, which affected every aspect of Lebanon's future as a state and society, could not be publicly debated. In 1992 three ministers declared: "We are not in Sweden . . . The function of the media is to direct public opinion, and to convey correct views."[21] Against bitter opposition, Hariri aimed to reduce the plethora of radio and television stations to a maximum of about five companies, one owned by the state and the others either owned by himself or under strict regime supervision. Parliamentary Speaker Barri and Interior Minister Michel al-Murr expected to have a major stake in two of these companies, thereby blending reduction of the media with money making.

Beneath what Michel Aoun derisively termed a "Syrian ceiling," civil society exhibited some resilience. The fact that Syria wanted to balance a number of elements in Lebanese politics meant that it did not always back the regime, particularly over media matters. For example, Hizballah had a special value for Syria as a "card" in Arab-Israeli affairs and in relations with the U.S.—unlike Aounism it did not frontally challenge Syrian interests and Damascus had no intention of fulfilling American expectations for its suppression in the absence of a satisfactory final peace with Israel. Hizballah thus had an autonomous political status provided it behaved itself, and its media enjoyed some immunity from regime pressure.

Generally Syria preferred a slow sapping of Lebanese civil society rather than regime assaults liable to provoke sharp resistance and embarrassments with foreigners. Up to the late 1990s Hariri's government behaved carefully toward private educational institutions and was unable to bring trade unions to heel. Public protests were effectively countered with detentions, emergency regulations, and curfews, but the union movement retained the capability to stage occasional general strikes. What really curtailed civil society was the falling income of the mass of Lebanese—beneath the upper bourgeois level most people had fewer and fewer resources to educate their children or to participate in social activities.

The manipulation of politics by the regime and Syria reached its apotheosis in the farcical 1996 parliamentary elections.[22] The government even overrode Lebanon's Constitutional Council when the council disallowed the electoral law because of the geographical gerrymandering of constituencies. The elections were stretched out over five weeks in August and September to facilitate laundering of the vote, with most results "fixed" by the cobbling together of official coalitions under Syrian oversight. Systematic irregularities—vote-buying, switching of ballot boxes, fraudulent votes on behalf of the dead and emigrants, detentions of opposition supporters, importation of thousands of "new citizens" from Syria into the north and the Biqa'—decisively disadvantaged many critics of the regime. Out of 128 seats, Hizballah held nine and other opponents of the government also took nine, an allotment preprogrammed by Syria for the sake of "flavor"[23] and cosmetic cover. Exploiting the dependence of part of the population on state services,[24] the political leadership managed to achieve a turnout of about 44%. It should be noted that for many Lebanese, sliding real incomes produced a combination of prostration and fury in attitudes toward the regime. Finally, factional groupings in the new parliament were largely determined by competitive personal interests, and had little to do with the concerns of the Lebanese people.

In May 1995 the weekly newsmagazine *al-Wasat* published results of a sample survey that indicated that about 70% of Lebanese opposed the entire conduct (*nahj*) of the Ta'if regime.[25] A similar survey at the same time in the newspaper *al-Nahar* showed that the top public priorities involved treatment of deteriorating living conditions and withdrawal of "foreign forces,"[26] a code-term for Syria. There was a deep rift between politicians and people across all the communities. In the Beirut governorate, for example, where Sunni Prime Minister Hariri stood for parliament in 1996, only 30% of electors bothered to vote, implying a very low turnout among Sunnis. Hariri's most solid support came from the Armenians. Maronites in particular felt alienated from every aspect of Lebanon's new order, in which most of them saw the Syrians and some Muslims as the victors and themselves as the vanquished.

After the 1996 elections one observer[27] criticized opposition groups for not producing a proper program to set against Hariri's "reconstruction," and for not establishing a coherent organization. However, the only possible opposition program would have involved tackling the main issues of "foreign forces" and the political and economic oppression of the bulk of the population, and the long-term reconciliation of confessional sensitivities with numerical democracy ("abolition of political sectarianism"). Such a program would have required the overthrow of the whole Ta'if regime, which was the agent of a foreign power and an exploitative local elite, and which operated according to a written definition of sectarian political allocations, unlike the oral understandings of the 1943–89 "National Pact" regime. Under Hariri, as during and before the war years, public morality did not exist and politics simply consisted of cynical maneuvers; in October 1996 al-Wasat defined talk of an anti-corruption drive as nothing more than cover for removing some officials for other reasons.[28] In brief, Lebanon's "second republic" was a non-reformable carpetbagger operation.

By the late 1990s the state of affairs in Lebanon made organization of serious opposition as futile an endeavor as in Asad's Syria. The government tolerated and ignored shrill criticism of its corrupt and heavy-handed methods, provided the critics accepted the Ta'if system and did not breathe a word against Syria. Such critics were impotent and even serviceable in propaganda for foreign consumption about Lebanon's "democracy." If they became too persistent they could be threatened with judicial proceedings.

Opponents of the Ta'if system, however, risked ferocious repression. Michel Aoun's more active followers, though allowed to maintain a small and closely watched political association, were regularly persecuted and imprisoned after 1990, "tortured from time to time in the basements of the defense ministry and other places" according to Druze leader Walid Junblatt.[29] Further, the respected U.S.-based organization Human Rights Watch noted "kidnappings" of many Lebanese and Palestinians by the Syrian and Lebanese security services, their torture in the Syrian military intelligence headquarters in Beirut, and their transfer to Syria.[30] The Director of Human Rights Watch accused Prime Minister Hariri of "denying what everyone in his country knows to be true."[31] Syrian-Lebanese integration evidently worked well at the level of "gulags," with up to several hundred Lebanese held incognito in Syria in the mid-1990s.[32] Of course, a similar number of southern Lebanese Shi'is were detained by the

Israelis or by Israel's proxy militia, the South Lebanese Army.

On 13 October 1996 the regime's security forces disrupted a church service in the Kisrawan village of Hrajil, held in remembrance of Lebanese killed in the October 1990 Syrian assault on East Beirut, and reportedly dragged away participants while the priest was giving communion.[33] On 19 December 1996, after a gun attack on a Syrian minibus, the regime detained forty-eight East Beirut Christians, including the head of a human rights reporting group and a journalist for the leading Beirut daily *al-Nahar*. It was a classic secret police operation—raids on homes by plainclothes security personnel, no arrest warrants, no charges, and releases a week or two later.[34]

Even Shiʻi Islamists condemned such intimidation. Muhammad Husayn Fadlallah asserted that "we can construct our freedom according to a measure other than the freedom of intelligence agencies,"[35] and former Hizballah leader Subhi Tufayli demanded "the prosecution of officials responsible for the seizure of opponents [of the regime]."[36] The Islamists perceived clearly who might be the next target, if there were future difficulties between Syria and Iran. The best reflection on these circumstances, however, remained that of Ignatius IV Hazim, Orthodox patriarch of Antakya based in Damascus, who had remarked a year earlier: "all I know is that as long as we can go, come, meet, and even speak in our church, and perhaps just a little in our country, then we can count God's blessings."[37] Apparently, even this degree of freedom could not be guaranteed in the new Lebanon.

Toward the New Century

In the late 1990s there seems little reason for optimism about pluralist politics in Syria and Lebanon. Syria looks to a future either of unabated authoritarianism or of a chaotic decay of the Baʻthist regime. Lebanon, which has become Syria's satellite, retains some political diversity, in part for cosmetic purposes and in part because of a gradually declining resistance in its civil society. Coalescence between Syria and Lebanon since 1990 has reflected both Syrian power and the joint social and economic interests of the ruling class of the two countries. This coalescence has involved considerable tension, for the meantime repressed by the inter-linked security apparatuses.

First, Lebanon's "reconstruction" and Syria's "liberalization" have enabled part of the Lebanese and Syrian bourgeoisie to flourish while the majority of the population of the two countries hears about "growth" but experiences low or deteriorating living standards, in the context of increasingly dramatic skews in income distribution. Second, Lebanon's economic, political, and sectarian distinctiveness cannot be easily recon-ciled with an elite-driven integration (*takaamul*)[38] with its more powerful but in many respects less sophisticated neighbor, an integration for which the consent of the Lebanese people has been neither sought nor given. Third, Arab-Israeli developments, whether toward peace or military esca-lation, could well have destabilizing implications for the present Lebanese and Syrian regimes.

References

Harris, William, 1996. *Faces of Lebanon: Sects, Wars, and Global Extensions.* Princeton: Markus Wiener Publishers.

Lobmeyer, Hans, 1994. "*Al-dimuqratiyya hiyya al-hall*? The Syrian Opposition at the End of the Asad Era." In Eberhard Kienle, ed., *Contemporary Syria: Liberalization between Cold War and Cold Peace.* London: British Academic Press, pp. 81–96.

Middle East Watch, 1991. *Syria Unmasked: The Suppression of Human Rights by the Asad Regime.* New Haven: Yale University Press.

Perthes, Volker, 1994. "Stages of Economic and Political Liberalization." In Eberhard Kienle, ed., *Contemporary Syria: Liberalization between Cold War and Cold Peace.* London: British Academic Press, pp. 44–71.

Seale, Patrick, 1965. *The Struggle for Power in Syria.* London: Oxford Univer-sity Press.

Seale, Patrick, 1991. "Asad: Between Institutions and Autocracy." In Richard Antoun and Donald Quataert, eds., *Syria: Society, Culture, and Polity.* Albany: SUNY Press, pp. 97–110.

Notes

1. Seale, 1965, pp. 164–185.

2. Perthes in Kienle, 1994, p. 51.

3. Middle East Watch, 1991, pp. 85–87.

4. Perthes in Kienle, 1994, p. 65.

5. Seale in Antoun and Quataert, 1991, p. 98.

6. Middle East Watch, 1991, p. 79.

7. Middle East Watch, 1991, p. 87.

8. *Al-Hayat*, 24 July 1996, observes that 2,000 were freed in 1995, leaving 250 in detention.

9. Ibid.

10. Perthes in Kienle, 1994, p. 65; Lobmeyer in Kienle, 1994, p. 95.

11. Perthes in Kienle, 1994, p. 69.

12. *Al-Hayat*, 18 and 28 July 1996.

13. Estimates from Lebanon's General Security Directorate for arrivals in and departures from Lebanon give a high figure of 1.4 million Syrian workers for July 1995 (*al-Nahar*, 24 July 1995), whereas unnamed Syrian "experts" later asserted that their numbers never exceeded 450,000—and that "they do not benefit from the social insurance and security for foreign workers stipulated in the clauses of bilateral agreements, and this is the most important reason for their employment" (*al-Hayat*, 12 January 1997).

14. *Al-Hayat*, 16 August and 25 September 1996.

15. Harris, 1996, p. 268.

16. *Al-Safir*, 16 September 1991.

17. *Al-Wasat*, 7 August 1995.

18. *Al-Nahar*, 2 August 1995.

19. *Al-Nahar*, 19 July 1995.

20. Arabic text in *al-Nahar*, 7 September 1991. English translation in *The Lebanon Report*, October 1991.

21. *Al-Anwar*, 29 April 1992.

22. Harris, 1996, pp. 321–322.

23. Walid Shuqayr in *al-Hayat*, 5 September 1996.

24. This factor is excellently explained by Michael Young in *The Lebanon Report*, Fall 1996, p.25.

25. *Al-Wasat*, 8 May 1995.

26. *Al-Nahar*, 16 May 1995.

27. Michael Young in *The Lebanon Report*, Fall 1996, p. 25.

28. *Al-Wasat*, 21 October 1996. "Opening the corruption file 'means¡ a temporary probity for the sake of reshuffling the distribution of 'bureaucratic¡ quotas (*Icadat tawzica al-hisas*).

29. *Al-Safir*, 7 December 1992. Junblatt himself moved close to the brink with Damascus in November 1996, then carefully stepped back after clear warnings: "Some senior Syrian officials repeat that Junblatt's attacks on the 'Lebanese¡ prime minister 'have become aimed at us, not at Hariri' . . . 'and¡ consider that his signing of the 'banner and information' petition presented by the organizers of tomorrow's public demonstration against government policy represents a big escalation against Damascus, especially as his signature appears together with the signatures of people well-known for their hostility to Syria and to its role and policy in Lebanon" (*Al-Hayat*, 27 November 1996, Walid Shuqayr column). It should be noted here that Hariri's government had banned public demonstrations since 1993.

30. *Al-Hayat*, 24 October 1996.

31. Ibid.

32. In an interview with *al-Hayat* (10 January 1997), Michel Aoun observed that "everyone knows there are hundreds of Lebanese detainees in Syria."

33. *Al-Hayat*, 14 October 1996, reporting an opposition communiqué. The government responded almost a week later with an unconvincing denial (*al-Hayat*, 19 October 1996). Apparently the detentions were not restricted to the forty-eight in East Beirut—after a small explosion near a Syrian military intelligence facility in Tripoli on 17 December 1996, there were reports of arrests of dozens of Tripoli Sunnis (*The Lebanon Report*, Winter 1996).

34. I spoke by telephone with one of the detainees on 29 December 1996, after his release. Because his conversations were probably being monitored, he could only describe his detention in indirect language—that he had been "away for a week."

35. *Al-Hayat*, 8 January 1997.

36. *Al-Hayat*, 11 January 1997.

37. *Al-Nahar*, 14 October 1995.

38. After signing a set of Syrian-Lebanese economic agreements in Damascus in mid-January 1997, Lebanese Prime Minister Hariri stated that meetings would continue "for the good of the one people in the two sisterly countries"

until "integration between the two countries" (*al-Hayat*, 21 January 1997). Use of the word *takaamul* plainly delighted the Syrians. This word did not appear in the 1989 Ta'if agreement or even in the 1991 Syria-Lebanon "Brotherhood Treaty." It represented a return to the language of the 1986 "tripartite agreement," a failed Syrian diktat involving the main Lebanese militias of the time. Hariri had absolutely no Lebanese mandate for proceeding toward *takaamul*.

Re-Inventing Nationalism in Ba'thi Iraq 1968–1994: Supra-Territorial and Territorial Identities and What Lies Below

AMATZIA BARAM

I. From Egalitarian-Integrationist to Iraqi-Centered Pan-Arabism

A few months after they came to power in Iraq in July 1968, the radically pan-Arab Ba'th Party started showing signs of growing fascination with Iraq's particular pre-Islamic and pre-Arab past. As suggested in a study of the ideology and culture of the Ba'th regime of Iraq, in order to avoid undue criticism from within the party, as well as from pan-Arab circles outside of Iraq during the first, unstable years of their rule, the infant regime chose to introduce its new credo through a purely cultural, rather than an explicitly political, campaign.[1] In hindsight, in view of his unmatched devotion to this idea, there may be no doubt that the prime moving force behind this campaign was a young and obscure party security chief, one Saddam Husayn al-Nasiri al-Tikriti, a relative and protégé of President Ahmad Hasan al-Bakr.

Since 1968–1969 Iraqi artists, poets, novelists, and playwrights have been encouraged to derive their inspiration from the civilizations and cultures that flourished in Mesopotamia-Iraq from remote antiquity to the modern age. These included, of course, the Islamic civilization of the 'Abbasid Caliphate (its Persian component played down) but, also, and conspicuously, the pagan civilizations of Sumer, Akkad, Babylon, Assyria, and Chaldea–New Babylon. In addition, the state started gradually to introduce ancient Medieval-Islamic, but also Mesopotamian, cultural festivals, as well as names to the administrative map of Iraq and the various state institutions, with the result that by the end of the 1970s long-vanished pre-Islamic and medieval Islamic places' and personal names like Babylon, Nineveh, Sumer, Uruk, Tammuz, Ishtar, Gilgamesh, Qadisiyya, and al-Anbar became by necessity household names in Ba'thi Iraq.

Since the late 1970s the Iraqi people have been encouraged to see themselves not only as the cultural heirs of their Semitic Mesopotamian predecessors, but also as their genetic "offspring". While this claim cannot be easily dismissed, the Ba'th regime went one step further when it endeavored to effectively Arabize the ancient Mesopotamians through an extensive campaign of rewriting history. That this new "Ba'thi approach in studying history and in writing and analyzing its events," as Saddam once put it,[2] left the Kurds out in the cold was a small price to pay. Likewise all Iraqis were encouraged to regard themselves as superior to other Arabs, and thus as deserving a leadership role. This approach was crowned by an RCC communiqué issued on the day of the invasion of Kuwait: "Oh great Iraqi people, pearl of the Arabs' crown and symbol of their might and pride."[3]

Since Saddam Husayn became president in 1979, the "Mesopotamian" trend became inseparable from an unprecedented cult of personality. The young president, embodying the whole Iraqi people, was depicted as the heir and equal, indeed, sometimes superior to great Mesopotamian figures like Sargon the Akkadian, Nebuchadnezzar, Hammurabi, and Sannecherib, and some affinity was implied between him and mythological figures like Gilgamesh and the Sumero-Akkadian god of fertility and resurrection, Dumuzi-Tammuz.

The stress on the Iraqi identity and superiority was an unmistakable departure from Ba'th party orthodoxy, which stressed the egalitarian and amalgamative nature of the future Arab unity, meant to lead eventually to the disappearance of the existing Arab peoples within an all-Arab crucible. Thus, rather than a shift to Iraqi isolationism, Ba'th fascination with the glory that was Mesopotamia was, in fact, part of a shift to a different, Iraqi-centered brand of pan-Arabism. Indeed, since spring 1979, to suppress any expectations of an integrative Iraqi-Syrian union, Saddam

Husayn started to preach explicitly for a change in party doctrine. Rather than integrative unity which had been proved unworkable, he argued, the party should strive to establish in the Arab world a loose federation. This way each individual Arab people and state could preserve its separate identity forever.[4]

It has been suggested that this shift was the result of growing realization that the traditional doctrine of the Baʿth presented a lethal threat to the fledgling Baʿth regime in Baghdad. Rather than consolidating their hold on power, they risked getting prematurely embroiled in and exhausted by pan-Arab affairs (the Arab-Israeli conflict, permeation of Baʿthi influence from Damascus and Nasirite influence from Cairo). Also, an integrationist agenda was unpopular with the Kurds and, more importantly, with many Shiʿis.[5]

Despite later shifts of emphasis in national ideology and practice, not least importantly an extensive process of pretended Islamization, the Baʿth regime and the man at the helm never relinquished their attachment to Iraq's great pre-Islamic past. This was still the case despite the apparent contradiction between the newly-discovered Islamic piety and fondness for Jahili pagan cultures. Thus, for example, during the Kuwait crisis, to prove Iraq's right to Kuwait, Saddam Husayn explained to leaders of Arab trade unions:

> you know as Arabs that Iraq's civilization is 6000 years old. Is it possible for a civilization which is 6000 years old to have been isolated from the sea?[6]

Iraqi artists continued to draw their inspiration from ancient Mesopotamian art.[7] Postage stamps depicting Mesopotamian civilizations continued to appear regularly.[8] The state continued to produce documentaries connected with ancient Iraq, usually with some reference to the president's place in Mesopotamian history.[9] "Mesopotamian" Festivals were still being celebrated.[10] Numerous poems and a few novels using Mesopotamian themes were still being written.[11] Even playwrights continued to compose variations on the theme of Gilgamesh.[12]

The last important exposition to date of what may be termed "the Mesopotamian trend" in the Baʿthi national credo in Iraq came in Saddam Husayn's July 17th Revolution Day speech of 1994. In his attempt to impress his listeners with the renaissance of Iraq and its people under himself and the Ba'th, Saddam Husayn equated the party, and by implication himself, with the god Dumuzi-Tammuz, who dies every year in the fall and is reborn in the spring with the new vegetation:

> Some 5000 years ago, the Iraqis produced Tammuz, the man [?] and the leader, who took good care of the needs of his people . . . They greatly honored him and placed him in the highest possible rank in life in accordance with the standards of that time [declaring him god] . . . The people called Tammuz the Virtuous Son [al-Ibn al-Barr, the translation from Sumerian of the name Du-mu-zi]. Since the . . . July 1968 Revolution, Tammuz returned to the field of responsibility . . . after a long absence . . . of 700 years . . . Tammuz returned as a leader of the people and a Virtuous Son. Tammuz is back to protect the weak from themselves [to save the Shi'a and the Kurds from their own revolutionary and destructive instincts?] . . . to nourish the elements of virtue in their minds, and to straighten the elements of weakness and evil within them. He is back to protect them from the others, the wolves of the foreigner and the wolves of their [own] kin, who do not refrain from sin . . . Tammuz is back, a faithful son of the people and the country and a wise, experienced leader with his new principles, adopted by his glorious revolution of . . . July 1968. . . . You have proven for over 3000 years that you are a loyal people. You have given Dumuzi-Tammuz the trait of a Faithful Son and you highly cherished him . . . [The Iraqis] are qualified to play their [leading] role within the [Arab] nation.[13]

Even before the radical shift to Islam, the result was a somewhat baffling ideological and cultural cocktail of secular pan-Arabism, Iraqi nationalism based largely on pagan civilizations, and some lip-service to Islam. But, between the early seventies and the beginning of the Iraq-Iran War in 1980, there was no mistaking where the main emphasis was placed: secularism, Arab-Iraqi identity, and Iraqi interests.

II. The Islamic Component

A. The Genesis of the Ba'th: Islam in the Thought of Michel 'Aflaq

In theory, as it was formulated in the 1940s by Michel 'Aflaq, co-founder and the then-unchallenged leading ideologue of the Ba'th party, the Ba'th preached for *'ilmaniyyat al-dawla*, "a secular state."[14] For 'Aflaq, a Greek Orthodox Christian by birth, secularism offered the best chance of integration within the largely Muslim Arabic-speaking community of his homeland Syria. But 'Aflaq needed also to make sure that his fledgling movement would strike roots in the much larger community of Syrian and other Arab Muslims. As implied by his speeches, strict adherence to secularism, let alone atheism, and ignoring Islam altogether, threatened to severely restrict the party's public appeal.

'Aflaq called upon all Arabs, Muslims as well as Christians, to admire Islam and the Prophet because of Islam's "important role in shaping Arab history and Arab nationalism." Yet, to balance this tribute to Islam he stressed that it should be admired [only] "as a spiritual movement which became inseparable from Arab history [and which became] colored with their ingenuity and enabled their renaissance." The special place of Islam in 'Aflaq's thinking, thus, was spiritual, and he warned that it "should not be imposed." 'Aflaq emphasized time and again that the Ba'th "movement" is against atheism (*al-ilhad*), and that "it is impossible to separate it from religion" but, in the same breath, he warned that the movement is opposed to "the widespread religiosity" which represents "shallow, false faith." 'Aflaq's Ba'th was "looking at the various religions as equal, respecting and revering them equally." As 'Aflaq described it, the secularization of the state will "free religion from [the influence of] political circumstances" and thus enable it to flourish and exert positive moral influence on people. Thus, the state as such should be "based on a social foundation, Arab nationalism, and a moral one: freedom," rather than on any particular religion.[15] 'Aflaq may have been a religious person, but the religiosity he offered his disciples, most of whom were young Muslims who went through the secular educational system of the Syrian state, was ethereal, theoretical, and devoid of specific substance:

Maybe we [Ba'this] are not seen praying with the ones who pray, or fasting with the ones who fast, but we believe in God because we are in dire need and painful yearning for Him: our burden is heavy, our road arduous, and our destination is faraway.[16]

It seems that 'Aflaq believed that he had placed all the necessary ideological safety valves to prevent the Islamization of party ideology and practice. In hindsight, however, unlike thoroughly secular Christian-Arab ideologues like Antun Sa'adah and Qustantin Zurayq, or the pan-Arab proto-Ba'thi 'Alawite Zaki Arsuzi, 'Aflaq did leave in his wake a great deal of ambiguity.[17] As will be shown below, soon before his death or a few days afterwards this ambiguity eventually caught up with him.

B. Saddam Husayn: The Early Years

In late 1977, in a programmatic lecture following the most severe Shi'i riots since the party came to power,[18] Deputy RCC Chairman Saddam Husayn returned to 'Aflaq. He warned against "atheism" (*al-ilhad*), but also against any attempt to imitate the religious parties and mix religion and politics: "We should go back to the origin of our ideology, [namely:] to be proud of religion, without, [however], adopting policies for religion." "Our party," he exclaimed, "is with [religious] faith (*al-iman*), but it is not a religious party, nor should it be one." In line with this tenet of faith, since 1979–80 the party has strongly denounced Khomeini's "politicization of religion by the state." For a number of tactical reasons, Saddam Husayn rejected altogether the possibility of applying the *shari'a* in all walks of life, as demanded by the fundamentalists:

To follow **the reactionary line** by building the theory of modern life and its development on the teachings of **ancient jurisprudence,** would lead Muslims to differences which would consequently turn into conflict because of existing differences between [the Sunni and Shi'i] sects . . . In so doing we would provide the proper atmosphere for neo-colonialism to play its malicious game . . . dividing the people. [emphasis added][19]

In another lecture he went much further than mere tactical considerations, implying that the Ba'th came to replace Islam in the modern age:

> Islam is the soul of the Arab nation. However, we derive
> from the history of our nation . . . lessons, especially of Islam,
> to **express in a new theory**—the Arab Ba'th Socialist Party—
> the . . . [nation's] spirit and its orientation towards revolution,
> progress and social construction. [emphasis added][20]

> Even if there were one faith [in Iraq, and] . . . coherence
> between [the Sunni and Shi'i] sects, we should not force our
> treatment of the present worldly aspects of life into a frame-
> work of religious jurisprudence. **The current social problems
> . . . are quite different from those of the early Islamic times,
> when the rules of jurisprudence were laid down . . . [These
> rules] cannot be the rule of present life.** [emphasis added][21]

Saddam Husayn must have known that the differences in substantive
law between the Sunna and the Shi'a are minor, and that thus Islamic legislation could hardly impair patriotic unity. And, indeed, he revealed that
his much more pressing fear was that, if they made meaningful concessions to Islam, his party and regime might lose their identity and distinction, and thus face an ideological crisis. The result would be that the con-
fused membership and public alike would no longer be able to tell the difference between the Ba'th and the fundamentalists, and the party would
lose power.[22]

As the Iraqi vice president saw it, going religious is a mistaken policy also because the Ba'th had no chance of beating the religious parties at
their own game:

> You will not even succeed through tactics of pretending to
> follow the reactionary force . . . adopting its understanding of
> the relations between the state and religion. **The religious
> forces of reaction will take over the leadership in such a
> case, because every . . . ideology has its own leaders** . . .
> leaders from reactionary circles . . . are more specialized in
> this field [emphasis added].[23]

Throughout the series of lectures Saddam Husayn radiated a sense of foreboding. He implied that the majority of the Iraqis were more traditional than the party, and thus that the latter's secular policy may not be popular with many. There was need, he said, to "convince the whole people and transform them" along the party line; there is need to "enhance the leading role of our party in moving and transforming and directing society"; and he cautioned his party members that possibly "the majority of your people" might "stand with the . . . [religious reactionary] minority." In such a case, he advised, "you have to act skillfully," by refraining from offending the sensitivities of the masses. All the same, however, Saddam Husayn instructed the party cadres: "[You must not] give up your . . . leadership in . . . education." "Ambiguity . . . should not be our means of winning over the majority." [24]

C. Under Ba'th Rule: The Search for a Sunni-Shi'i Common Denominator and the Islamization of Party Rhetoric

In reality, however, things were more complex. After they came to power for the second time in July 1968, the Ba'th regime showed deference to Islam on many levels of state activity. It appeared, essentially, in two interrelated forms. One was through tribute to Shi'i Islam, the religion of the disempowered majority. Another was through the demonstration of Islamic piety in general. This was designed to win some popularity among traditional circles in the Sunni population but also, no less importantly, among the Shi'a in the poorer quarters of Baghdad and in the south, widely considered to be the more traditional segment of Iraqi society.

Since the mid-1970s, the state has nationalized a number of Shi'i festivals and mourning days: to an extent the 'Ashura', and more effectively the birthdays of Imams 'Ali and al-Husayn. On the latter occasions the state, the party, or the Ministry of Awqaf would organize the celebrations. The president would send his representative to the celebrations in Najaf and Karbala, and would read the president's message, promising to continue to sponsor the Shi'i holy places. Usually these messages would praise the two Imams as Islamic and Arab heroes and the defenders of faith and justice. Occasionally they would go one step further, severely denouncing the Umayyads. They would forge a link between the latter and the present regime of Hafiz al-Asad in Damascus, while emphasizing the bond between the Iraqi regime and the two Imams and their legacy.[25] During the Iran-Iraq War it was Ayat Allah Khomeini who was accused of reneging on all the ideals upheld by the two Imams, and Saddam Husayn was hailed as the one who defended them.[26] Occasionally the ʿAshura' mourning was defined as applying to all the country's governorates, thus making it a part of the all-Iraqi, rather than a particularly Shiʿi identity.[27] Furthermore, sometimes people identified with the regime would even define the territory of Iraq (and thus by implication, Iraqi territorial nationalism) in terms of the resting place of these two great Imams and other Shiʿi saints.[28]

Since he became president, on various all-Islamic and particularly Shiʿi occasions in the holy places, Saddam Husayn was identified as the offspring of the two Imams and of the Prophet. This way the regime sought to create a fusion between the leader, the people, the soil, and what was intended to appear as an ecumenical faith. Thus, for example, upon al-Husayn's birthday in 1987, the daily newspaper of the Ministry of Defense announced in a headline over a whole page: "Karbala Is Celebrating the Birthday of Imam Husayn, Grandfather (*jadd*) of Leader Saddam Husayn," and another page-wide headline: "Tremendous [Popular] Pride in the Sponsorship of al-Husayn's Grandson (*hafid*) of the Holy Places and [Karbala], the City of Jihad and Sacrifice."[29]

This identification with the Shiʿi Imams may not have been, however, as problematic as it may seem: after all, many Sunnis are very critical of the Umayyads (excluding ʿUmar ibn ʿAbd al-ʿAziz) for their lack of religiosity, and ʿAli (the fourth *khalifa*) is admired by all. Al-Husayn, the Prophet's grandson, too, is loved by many. This way, by supporting the two Imams and incorporating them into the Iraqi national pantheon, the regime could demonstrate empathy towards the Shiʿa without, however, alienating the Sunna.

On the all-Islamic level, since the party came to power and throughout its rule the state "nationalized" the main occasions: *ʿId al-fitr*, *ʿId al-adha*, *Iftar* dinners during Ramadan, Badr Day, *Laylat al-Israʿ wal-Miʿraj*, *Laylat al-Qadar*, and similar events.[30] In terms of the approach to Islam, the most important contribution of the Iraq-Iran War to party ideology was a quantum jump in Islamic rhetoric. Expressions like "A secular state" disappeared. On the eve of the war the most important party organ still called for "secularism" and strongly denounced Khomeini's "politicization of religion by the state."[31] However, during the war the regime's propaganda quickly shifted toward a different approach: the Ba'th regime and Saddam Husayn were upheld as "our historical, ingenious, Jihad-launching leadership, fighting for the future of our Iraqi people and elevating our monotheistic Islamic religion, guided by the message of eternal Islam" (an interesting variation on 'Aflaq's secular "Eternal Message").[32] Khomeini was depicted as "the Big Imposter" (*al-dajjal al-kabir*), or just "the Impostor," Khamene'i and Rafsanjani were branded "the Small Impostors." The Iranian regime was defined as *kuffar*, "the Impostors of Qomm and Tehran" and "enemies of Allah, Mankind, and history." They were accused of "attacking the unity of all the Muslims and the teachings of the Islamic *shari'a*," of "apostasy" (*ridda*), and of "black hatred towards Arabism and Islam." Khomeini's regime was branded "the regime of the barbarians (*al-jahla*) and illiterates in Tehran."[33] And while the Iraqis and their leader were defined as "offspring" of the Prophet and his jihad warriors, Khomeini and his "tyrannical clique (*al-fia al-baghiya*)" were dubbed "offspring of Kisra and Rustam," or even as "Zoroastrians" and "Magian priests" (*majus*).[34] Indeed, thematically a new concept was introduced (or rather fully elaborated and accentuated), namely that the Arabs are the leaders of Islam. In an attempt to drive a wedge between the Shi'i Arabs of Iraq and the Iranian Shi'a, the Ba'th regime endeavored to convince its Shi'a that, because the Prophet was an Arab, the Qur'an was given to mankind in Arabic on Arab soil, and the Arabs were the first carriers of Islam, Persians ought to recognize Arab seniority. Not surprisingly, these principles were fully elaborated for the first time in a presidential speech to ulama and "men of religion" in Najaf and Karbala.[35]

In terms of *shar'i* legislation, too, the Ba'thi state was less than wholly faithful to its original principles: following in the footsteps of the 'Arif regime, some *shar'i* rules, partially forbidding "public fast-breaking" (*al-iftar al-'alani*) during the daytime, were occasionally announced in Ramadan. To placate the Shi'a, some limitations on public entertainment were imposed during the first ten days of Muharram.[36] According to interviews, the Ramadan rules were imposed more strictly during the last years of the Iraq-Iran War than ever before. Another important sphere of legislation is personal status. The Ba'th inherited the Law of Personal Status, a combined legacy of the Law introduced under Qasim (1959) and amended by the first Ba'th regime (1963). This law deviated only very little from the *shari'a*. Mainly in 1978 the second Ba'th regime introduced minor changes to improve women's status.[37] At the same time, however, until close to the end of the Iraq-Iran War there was no other *shar'i* or pseudo-*shar'i* legislation. Thus, for example, the Penalty Code remained a secular one. Likewise, when in 1977 a new Law of Reforming the Legal System (*qanun islah al-nizam al-qanuni*) was introduced, the law-makers aspired to give in it expression only to "socialist values, Arab nationalism and democracy," with Islam (and religion in general) left out.[38] In the same vein, continuing a long tradition in the Iraqi state, the Ba'th regime occasionally introduced amendments to Liquor Law (*qanun al-mashrubat al-ruhiyya*) No. 3 of 1931, regulating (but allowing) the public sale and consumption of spirits.[39]

D. Islamic Rhetoric in the Kuwait Crisis and the Gulf War

Close to the end of the Iraq-Iran War a non-*shar'i* law, presented by some as a *shar'i* one, was enacted which "gave men the right to kill their sisters, wives, etc. if they commit adultery or any other crimes of passion."[40] The second sign of change appeared when, in June 1989, Baghdad announced the death of Michel 'Aflaq. In its communiqué on this occasion the pan-Arab and the Regional-Iraqi Leaderships of the Ba'th party announced that "the late 'Aflaq . . . embraced Islam as his religion [prior to his death]."[41] As disclosed to this author by a Western diplomat who served in Iraq at the time, 'Aflaq's family was unaware of his conversion.[42]

During the crisis of Kuwait Saddam Husayn's speeches and Iraq's war propaganda in general became progressively more Islamic. As the regime apparently saw it, this held the promise of appealing to the deepest sentiments of most Iraqis, and shoring up Islamic support on the international arena. During the crisis the Iraqi president added a new dimension to Iraqi-Arab nationalism when he placed Iraq in the center of three concentric circles: "the Arab nation," "the Islamic world," and Mankind as a whole. Islam and the Arabs, he argued, are in crisis. The moral corruption of the rich Gulf Arabs and the presence of foreign, "infidel" troops on the holy soil of Arabia are only two indications of this crisis. God has chosen the Arabs, led by Iraq, [led by Saddam Husayn,] to save Islam, then spread it throughout the world, and thus lead Mankind to "real happiness." This was Iraq's mission in the Kuwait crisis.[43]

The Islamization of the regime's symbolism was complete when, on January 14, one day before the UN ultimatum was to elapse, the president "ordered that the phrase 'God is great' be added to the Iraqi flag."[44] Accordingly, on the first birthday of the Ba'th party after the war the president announced: "[The Ba'th is] the party of Arabism and Islam!"[45]—thus leaving out not only the Kurds, but also the Christians, the Yazidis, the Mandeans and others.

E. Enter Shari'a

Following the Iraqi withdrawal from Kuwait, the military defeat, the bloody suppression of the Shi'i Uprising (*Intifadat Sa'ban*) of March 1991 and the worsening economic conditions, Saddam Husayn initiated a series of Islamization steps in the educational, institutional, and most importantly (and the only one to be discussed here) legal spheres. During 1993–1994 the Iraqi press gave expression to a deep sense of social, economic, and political crisis: a massive wave of violent crime, private entrepreneurs ignoring the government price policies, widespread corruption within the administration, and growing frustration even at the highest echelons at their inability to curb inflation and stabilize the economy.[46] On May 29, 1994 it was announced that a new government was formed, under the premiership of the president himself. The announcement made it clear that this unusual step was made necessary by the economic crisis and the sheer decline of the Iraqi dinar.[47] A few days later the Revolutionary Command Council, the highest decision- and lawmaking body, enacted Decree No. 59 of June 4, 1994, the first in a host of *shar'i* laws, with the result that the Iraqi Penal Code was completely transformed. According to the new law, with some minor exceptions, the punishment for robbery and car theft would be amputation of the right hand at the wrist. "In case of repetition the left foot should be amputated at the ankle."[48]

The next day the Minister of Awqaf commended the new law, explaining that its advantages accrued from it being "in line with God's Book and the provision of the Islamic law and in harmony with God's words: 'As to the thief, male or female, cut off his or her hands, a punishment by way of example from God . . . and God is exalted in power.'"[49] To avoid confusion between a war hero who lost a limb and a common thief, on August 18 the RCC issued Decree No. 109 to the effect that any thief whose hand was amputated "shall be tattooed between his eyebrows."[50] There was no attempt to present this as part of the *shariʿa*. Eventually, the list of offenses for which one was to lose one's hand was expanded to the breaking of practically every economic regulation. To drive home the notion that the law was fully enforced the Iraqi TV showed people with amputated, blood-dripping hands.[51] This was an indication that the regime saw in the new laws another, highly potent means to further terrorize its fear-stricken population and dissuade it from breaking the progressively more arbitrary economic regulations. Another indication in the same vein was provided when, in August 1994, the RCC decreed a clearly non-Islamic punishment, the amputation of an ear and tattooing for shirking military service and desertion. A doctor who refused to carry out this punishment was to lose a hand and be tattooed as well.[52]

One month later the RCC moved one step further when they promulgated Decree No. 82 of July 7, 1994. It stipulated the closure of all places of entertainment, discotheques, and night-clubs. Even though alcoholic drinks were still available on sale in special shops, the public consumption of such drinks was banned.[53] Not surprisingly, most of the Iraqi media, notably leading clergy, supported the Decree for bringing the Iraqi people back to Islam (thus implying that beforehand people and leadership had deviated from the right path).[54] In reality, however, it seems that Saddam Husayn had at least one motive that had little to do with Islam: the vast majority of Iraqis could not afford whisky anyway. But the extreme public frustration at the sight of the ostentatious extravagance of the few rich and powerful had to be contained. At the same time, however, the Iraqi president knew that outlawing spirits altogether would cause outrage even in a dispirited and tamed Baʿth party. That introducing the new criminal and liquor laws under an Islamic garb was deemed expedient indicates that, rightly or wrongly, Saddam Husayn viewed Islam as a potent force in his country's society.

Even the truncated new alcoholic drinks decree, however, became highly unpopular with some. This fact found expression in the daily *Babil*, the mouthpiece of 'Udayy Saddam Husayn. While the paper supported the amputation and tattooing decrees, and even demanded more, an editorial criticized the new prohibition policy severely. It argued that Iraqi Islam has always been reasonable, and that an attempt to turn Baghdad into Riadh is a serious mistake.[55] Only the president's son could voice such vehement opposition to Saddam Husayn's policy and get away with it. But in view of the social habits of the top echelons of party membership it is very likely that 'Udayy gave vent to frustration felt in these circles. The president and his government, as well as most of the media, however, presented things very differently: to them, Islam and much of what it entails became inseparable from the Iraqi-Arab national identity.

III. Tribalism Rediscovered

As admitted by Ba'thi sources and by Iraqi interviewees who lived for many years in the Shi'i south and the Kurdish north under Ba'th rule, tribal organization and affinities have not vanished from post-1958 Iraqi social and political life. As Ba'thi sources disclosed, despite the agrarian reform, many tribal shaykhs were still influential at least until the mid-1970s.[56] Indeed, Saddam Husayn himself admitted that in its difficult hour in March 1991, when the party disintegrated in the south in the face of the Shi'i Intifada, the regime was forced to turn to the tribal shaykhs for help because they had influence over their tribesmen.[57] This is not to say that the tribes have not gone through important changes, mainly as a result of a partial land reform, mass migration to the towns, the abolishing of the tribal legal autonomy, and the penetration of the central government to the countryside. Yet, it emerges from interviews with scions of shaykhly families that, in the rural areas, various forms of tribal groupings, under various forms and degrees of shaykhly authority, remained in existence. The Ba'th regime coexisted with the shaykhs and coopted those who were willing to cooperate. In the Kurdish north, tribal chiefs (many of whom were actually made chiefs by the regime) served as *mukhtars* and as military commanders (literally *mustashar*s, "advisers") in the fighting against the Kurdish nationalists.[58] No less, and probably more importantly, as pointed out by Hanna Batatu, tribal affinities continued to play an important role in the formation of Iraq's political elite under the 'Arif brothers (1963–68).[59] This was the case even more so under the Ba'th. As emerges from a number of interviews, since the early 1970s it has become common knowledge in Iraq that President Ahmad Hasan al-Bakr and Deputy Chairman of the RCC Saddam Husayn, as well as a few other key figures in the regime, were not only Tikritis, but also members of the Beygat, of the tribal federation of Albu Nasir (or Aal Nasir).

On the level of party doctrine, however, the approach to tribalism was highly critical. The Ba'th party has always preached for some kind of socialism and modernity, for secularism and all-Arab unity. Tribalism (*al-qabaliyya*, *al-'asha'iriyya*) was seen as diametrically opposed to all these revolutionary values.[60]

Since the suppression of the Shi'i *Intifada* in the south and the Kurdish revolt in the north in March–April 1991, the semi-covert support for tribal shaykhs and social organization became explicit and a conspicuous ingredient of Iraqi nationalism. This was not a completely arbitrary decision: during the 1991 revolt in the north the regime was still supported by some, if far fewer, Kurdish tribes. Less surprisingly, during the same revolt the regime was supported by Sunni Arab tribes.[61] In the south, according to both the revolutionaries and the regime, during the 1991 *Intifada* many Shi'i tribes remained on the sideline, and some even supported the regime.[62]

But the public overture to the tribal shaykhs stemmed also from a propaganda need. What on the surface seems to have been a divisive policy of encouraging tribal identities was, in fact, a device designed to obscure the traumatically divisive effect of the Shi'i revolt. By emphasizing the tribal makeup of Iraqi society the regime implied that the Shi'i-Sunni divide was a superficial one. As the regime's spokesmen had it, all Iraqis were united by tribalism. This, however, was mainly the case with Arabs, as occasionally the Kurds were implicitly excluded from the Iraqi sociocultural collective. Saddam Husayn went even further when he pointed out (correctly) that many a tribe in Iraq encompasses Sunni and

Shiʻi sections. Indeed, he claimed that even his own tribe had a Shiʻi branch.[63] The new policy was ushered in through high-profile visits by the president and his most senior lieutenants to tribal areas to meet with the shaykhs and their tribesmen, and return visits by the shaykhs to the capital to express their support and love for the president. Mass oath-taking by tribal chiefs, as well as letters of support for the president, became commonplace. Thus, for example, in a meeting between the president and 586 tribal chiefs and clergy from Babil (Hilla), they took an oath that embodied, in a bizarre cocktail, the three bases of political identification ushered in by Saddam Husayn since the late 1960s (apparently out of oversight omitting Arabism): the Mesopotamian, the Islamic, and the tribal.[64]

The regime distributed thousands of guns with ammunition to tribal shaykhs, and sometimes heavier weapons, accompanied by lavish financial allocations and other rewards. In return, the tribes were supposed to guard their areas against infiltrators.[65] Tribes were exposed (or re-activated) even in the capital city.[66] Also, since the late 1980s the tribal background of many senior party officials and senior army officers was revealed to the public, after many years during which this type of information had been suppressed.[67] While the tribes and their culture had not been ignored earlier,[68] since the late 1980s they have become an object of great academic and public interest.[69]

Saddam Husayn himself felt the need to harmonize the party's traditional approach with the new one. In a medal-awarding ceremony speech to tribal chiefs and internal security officers who fought "infiltrators" and "traitors" (in itself a sign of the new age of party-shaykhs cooperation), he made the astonishing announcement that "The Baʻth is the tribe of all the tribes" (ʻashirat kull al-ʻashaʼir).[70] Tribal values, or rather what the Iraqi leadership presented as such, became, all of a sudden, a legitimate part of Iraqi and Arab national political culture.[71]

The way in which party ideologues streamlined all these inconsistencies was not surprising: "Most" of the diverse "families and tribes and nationalities . . . and religious affinities" of Iraq "are adamant on holding together the front of the homeland" and are inseparably intertwined.[72] A Baʻthi ideologue tried to legitimize Saddam Husayn's tribal policies by announcing that, under the Baʻth, the tribes are no longer "tribal." Since the Ba'th revolution "There is no trace of the old negative aspects among the tribesmen."[73]

Clearly, this view was not shared by all in the Ba'th party. As with forbidding the public consumption of alcohol, here, too, by adding a new component to the national credo, the regime won, but also lost, some support. In a few articles in *Babil*, but also in the party daily, one could identify muffled protests against the return of tribalism to Iraq. Careful not to challenge the president directly, some partymen still expressed reservations. This is the case, for example, with objection to the central authorities' new respect for tribal custom in criminal cases.[74] A professor at the University of Basra reported that some tribal chiefs in the south are "sowing division" among the tribes by pursuing tribal feuds, rather than all-Iraqi unity. The writer demanded the party stop this "armed tribal inclination" (*al-naz'a al-'asha'iriyya al-musallaha*).[75] *Babil*, which showed the most consistent opposition to the president's tribal policy by giving publicity to intertribal armed clashes, commented wryly: "The tribes were given the weapons to fight the U.S. . . . not to fight among themselves."[76] Implying that the president's tribal policy could be used against Iraq, a journalist reported in the daily of the Ministry of Defense that Israeli and CIA researchers had recently taken great interest in the Iraqi tribes.[77]

IV. Conclusion

This account of the development and metamorphoses of regime-sponsored national ideology in Iraq under the Ba'th party is, in the first place, an account of political expediency and manipulation. While it seems that Saddam Husayn personally is deeply attached to Iraq's pre-Islamic history and to the military exploits of Islamic warriors, this fact is only of marginal importance. With minor exceptions, since 1968 he has been treating ideology as a tool designed to help enhance and perpetuate his rule. The shift of emphasis from egalitarian and integrationist to Iraqi-centered and imperial pan-Arabism during the 1970s was largely the result of a realization that deeper Iraqi involvement in Arab affairs was jeopardizing the very existence of the Ba'th regime in Baghdad. The growing emphasis on Shi'i values since the early 1970s resulted from a violent clash between the regime and the Shiʻi clergy mainly in the "Circles of Learning" in Najaf and Karbala, as the clergy and the Baʻth competed over the hearts and minds of the Shiʻi masses. Whether realistic or not, the fear of the potential influence of the ʻAlawite ruling elite in Damascus on the Iraqi Shiʻa, often implied by the regime's spokesmen since the mid-seventies, gave this trend additional impetus. The rise of Ayat Allah Khomeini to power in Tehran in 1979 further encouraged the regime to demonstrate great attachment to ʻAli and al-Husayn and their legacy. The Islamization of the regime's rhetoric, too, started in earnest soon after the victory of the Islamic Revolution in Tehran. By then, the regime felt the need to convince the people of Iraq that it was not, as claimed by Ayat Allah Khomeini, atheistic and an enemy of Islam. The Islamic rhetoric reached a climax during the excruciating months of the Kuwait crisis and Gulf War. And the fusion between Iraqi-Arab nationalism, *sharʻi* enactment, and tribal values occurred when the regime went through its most difficult tests: the Shiʻi and Kurdish revolts of spring 1991, and the oil embargo and its severe socioeconomic and political ramifications.

In summation, it has to be pointed out that, in addition to Saddam Husayn's cult of personality, despite all the shifting emphases there has been one hard ideological core that has remained constant since the early 70s: Iraqi-centered pan-Arabism. But so far this one constant has not been a viable one. In the future, too, while marginal Arab states like Yemen and Sudan might be willing to follow Iraqi-Baʻthi lead, it is difficult to imagine that major Arab countries like Egypt, Syria, or Saudi Arabia will ever be ready to do so. And so the only basis of political identification that has survived the ravages of time under the Baʻth is an ideological mirage.

No less importantly, the frequent and extreme shifts of ideological emphasis that come and go with the changing political circumstances indicate that, to Saddam Husayn's mind and to that of his lieutenants, even after 26 years of Baʻth rule, there was still no obvious common basis of political and cultural identification for the whole of the Iraqi people, or even for a majority within it. Finally, as reported to this author by an interviewee who left Iraq in 1990,[78] even before the Kuwait episode many Baʻthi old-timers were, and felt, left out. As they saw it, when Saddam

Husayn became president in 1979, intellectually inferior young opera-
tionists, devoid of any commitment to party ideals, took over. To those
old-timers even the deviations from party tenets of faith up to 1990 were
deeply frustrating. Having ended up, in the mid-1990s, with a more decisive return to a pseudo-Islamic and pseudo-tribal womb probably meant
to them an admission of the party's failure on all its main ideological bat-
tlefields. The party gave up its original integrationist pan-Arab vision,
and it severely limited the appeal of its new pan-Arabism by adopting an
Iraqi-centered credo. It gave up its secularism, and it relinquished its pre-
tense to integrationist Iraqi patriotism by embarking on neo-tribalism. But
seen from Saddam Husayn's perspective, all these changes were demonstrations of great flexibility and pragmatism (or cynicism, as the case may
be) designed to help him attain his main goal. Even though it is impossible to define the precise contribution of the Iraqi-centered, tribal, and religious policies to his survival, at this writing, despite his gross miscalcu-
lations on the international arena, Saddam Husayn was still ruling in
Baghdad. Thus, whatever the view of party old-timers of his ideological
acrobatics, the Iraqi president probably regards these acrobatics as part of
his successful strategy for staying alive and in power.

Notes

This article was written during my stay as a Fellow at the Woodrow Wilson
International Center for Scholars in Washington, D.C. in 1993–1994. Research
was aided by grants from the US Institute of Peace, Washington, D.C., the Bertha
Von Suttner Special Project for the Optimization of Conflicts, and Mr. Irving
Young. I am deeply indebted to all of the above for their invaluable help. I am
also grateful to my assistants Noga Efrati and Ronen Zeidel for their important
contributions.

1. Amatzia Baram, *Culture, History and Ideology in the Formation of Ba'thi
   Iraq, 1968–1989* (New York: St. Martin's Press, 1991), pp. 25–29.

2. Saddam Husayn, "On Writing History," in his *On History, Heritage and religion* (Baghdad: Translation and Foreign Languages Publishing House,
   1981), p. 9.

3. *Baghdad Voice of the Masses in Arabic*, Aug. 2, 1990, 0410 GMT, in *FBIS-*

NES, Aug. 2, 1990, p. 26. See also text of the party's pan-Arab leadership's communiqué *Baghdad Domestic Service in Arabic*, Aug. 3, 1990, in *FBIS-NES*, Aug. 3, 1990, pp. 28, 29.

4. Saddam Husayn in *Wa'i al-'Ummal*, February 17, 1979; *Afaq 'Arabiyya*, July, 1981, p. 32; The Ba'th Arab Socialist Party, *The Central Report of the Ninth Regional Congress, June 1982* (Baghdad), January 1983, p. 301; Saddam Husayn to *al-Tadamun* (Paris), February 4, 1988, and more.

5. Amatzia Baram, "Mesopotamian Identity in Ba'thi Iraq," *Middle Eastern Studies* 19, no. 4 (October, 1983), pp. 426–56; "Culture in the Service of Wataniyya: The Treatment of Mesopotamian-Inspired Art in Ba'thi Iraq," in *Asian and African Studies* 17 (Fall, 1983), pp. 265–313; *Culture, History and Ideology in the Formation of Ba'thist Iraq*, pp. 13–25.

6. *NA in Arabic*, Nov. 3, 1990, *FBIS-Serial JN0311165890*, p. 15.

7. See Layth Fattah al-Turk, son of the late Isma'il, one of the leading artists in modern Iraq who was deeply influenced by ancient local art, *al-'Iraq*, January 27, 1994. And Muris Haddad, "Enlil," "Sacrifices to the God Shamash," "Journey of Gilgamesh," "Ishtar," *al-'Iraq*, Feb. 9, 1994.

8. A new postage stamp depicting the ziggurat of Ur, *al-Qadisiyya*, February 5, 1994; commemorating the opening of the National Museum, a stamp with Sargon's head, *Alif Ba'*, Feb. 23, 1994.

9. "From Nebuchadnezzar to Saddam Husayn," to be screened by the Ministry of Education in all provinces, *al-Thawra*, Feb. 6, 1994.

10. The Babylon Festival was celebrated every year in September, and the Khadar Festival was resuscitated in 1994, *al-Thawra*, Feb. 18, 1994. For the Mosul Spring Festival, see *Babil*, April 8, 1992; *Alif Ba'*, ibid.

11. A recent example of a book is *The Sumerian*, by [the Shi'i] 'Abd al-Rahman al-Rubay'i, which won the first prize for fiction for 1993, *al-'Iraq*, Feb. 22, 1994.

12. *al-Thawra*, Sept. 10, 1992. And see two other productions of Gilgamesh in the Arab Drama Festival in Baghdad, by a theater from Basra, and another from Samawa, *Baghdad Observer*, April 8, 1992.

13. Baghdad Republic of Iraq Radio Network in Arabic, July 17, 1994, *FBIS Serial JN1707094594*, July 19, 1994.

14. Michel 'Aflaq, "al-'Arab Bayna Madihim wa Mustaqbalihim" (The Arabs Between their Past and Future), in his first collection of speeches *Fi Sabil al-Ba'th* (Beirut: Dar al-Tali'a, 1974), eleventh edition, p. 167. The speech was made in 1950.

15. Ibid., pp. 164–167.

16. "Dhikra al-Rasul al-'Arabi" (The Memory of the Arab Messenger), in *Fi Sabil al-Ba'th*, p. 134. The speech was made in the Syrian University, 1943.

17. For a succinct and penetrating discussion of the difficulties of the secular conception in the Islamic lands see P. J. Vatikiotis, *Islam and the State* (London and New York: Routledge, 1991, paperback edition), mainly pp. 72–99.

18. For a description of the development of the Husayni Processions (*al-mawakib al-husayniyya*) on *Yawm al-Arba'in* (the twentieth day of the month of Safar) into a symbol of Shi'i religiosity and anti-regime protest, see Amatzia Baram, "Two Roads to Revolutionary Shi'ite Fundamentalism in Iraq," in Martin E. Marty and R. Scott Appleby, *Accounting for Fundamentalism: The Dynamic Character of Movements* (Chicago: Univ. of Chicago Press and the American Academy of Arts and Sciences, 1994), pp. 556–559; and A. Baram, "The Radical Shi'i Movement of Iraq" in David Menashri, ed., *The Iranian Revolution and the Muslim World* (Boulder, San Francisco, Oxford: Westview Press, 1990), pp. 140–141.

19. Saddam Husayn's lecture "A View of Religion and Heritage," in his *On History, Heritage and Religion* (Baghdad: Translation and Foreign Languages Publishing House, 1981), pp. 24, 27–29. For his view on the application of the *shari'a*, see p. 29; for the approach to Khomeini's Islam see "Al-'Ilmaniyya wa Jawhar al-Mawqif al-Ba'thi Min al-Din," in *Al-Thawra al-'Arabiyya*, the internal party organ, disseminated to members only, July 1980, pp. 13–18.

20. Saddam Husayn, "On Writing History," in *On History, Heritage and Religion*, p. 13.

21. Saddam Husayn, "A View of Religion and Heritage," *On History, Heritage and Religion*, pp. 28–29.

22. Ibid., pp. 25–27.

23. Ibid., pp. 30–31.

24. Ibid., pp. 25, 35. See also p. 37.

25. For example: President Bakr's message on the occasion of the birthday of Imam 'Ali in Karbala on Sept. 27, 1969, in *Masirat al-Thawra fi Khutab wa Tasrihat al-Ra'is . . . 1968–1970* (Baghdad, 1971), pp. 132–3; Bakr on al-Husayn's birthday, ibid., pp. 136–138; *al-Jumhuriyya*, Oct. 9, 1970; *al-Jumhuriyya*, Sept. 6, 7, 1973; and *al-Thawra*, June 2, 12, 1981; and similar state-sponsorship of Imam 'Ali's birthday, *al-Jumhuriyya*, Oct. 3, 1969; *al-Thawra*, Aug. 25, 1972; *al-Jumhuriyya*, July 16, 1976; *al-Thawra*, May 22,

1981. For denunciation of the Umayyads and allusion to the contemporary regime in Damascus see, for example, *al-Jumhuriyya*, Jan. 23, 1975. And see *al-Thawra*, 10 Muharram, Nov. 7, 1981, where Yazid and the Umayyads are the embodiment of "prostitution" (*al-bagha*'); Saddam Husayn praying in Karbala to demonstrate "the interest and protection" of "the president and his deputy in the district of Karbala and its holy places" and "the Islamic leaders," and development plans, *al-Jumhuriyya*, Dec. 14, 1977.

26. For example, upon the 'Ashura', 'Alama al-Sayyid Kazim al-Kifa'i, a senior Shi'i 'alim, in Najaf, "All over again we are living in a war in the month of Muharram . . . in which Imam Husayn, ancestor of our Jihad Warrior Leader, fought against *kufr* and atheism . . . and this is what we see in the aggression of [Khomeini's] tyrannical clique," *al-Jumhuriyya*, September 26, 1985, 11 Muharram 1406; and similar expressions, 'Alama Sayyid Muhammad Mustafa Kalantar, and 'Alama Sayyid Jum'a al-Musawi, and Shaykh 'Abd al-Karim al-Sa'di, accusing the "Imposter" (or "Anti-Christ," *dajjal*) Khomeini of contradicting the teachings of al-Imam al-Sadiq that forbade a war between Muslims, and fighting on Muharram, Ibid. And see *al-Qadisiyya*, Oct. 18, 1983.

27. *al-Qadisiyya*, Oct. 18, 1983. The Ba'th also declared the tenth day of Muharram a national all-Iraqi holiday, but in this they followed the practice of previous regimes.

28. For example: Saddam Husayn to ulama in Karbala, *al-Thawra*, May 19, 1981; 'Abd al-Halim al-Sayyid 'Abd al-Karim, son of the late Ayat Allah 'Uzma al-Madani, a clergyman who preferred cooperation with the regime to defiance, *al-Jumhuriyya*, January 27, 1993; 'Izzat Ibrahim al-Duri, Deputy Chairman of the RCC in Karbala, *al-Qadisiyya*, February 18, 1987; *fatwa* by a group of ulama, defining Iraq as "the land of [pre-Islamic] civilization and Islamic Holy [Places] (*al-muqaddasat al-islamiyya*)," *al-Thawra*, May 2, 1981.

29. *al-Qadisiyya*, April 2, 1987; see also, for example, on the Prophet's birthday, defining Saddam Husayn as his "grandson," *al-Thawra*, August 19, 1994, in *FBIS-Serial JN2608161194*; "Pilgrims to Najaf," *al-Thawra*, November 8, 1981; the pilgrims in Karbala in a cable to the president, *al-Thawra*, 11 Muharram, Nov. 8, 1981, p. 6; Deputy RCC Chairman 'Izzat Ibrahim al-Duri in Najaf on 'Ali's birthday: "The heroic sons of the Twin Rivers under the leadership of the offspring of Imam 'Ali . . . are embodying these '[Ali's] principles with their pure blood in defense of the people . . . and the principles of the monotheistic religion," *al-Thawra*, March 4, 1988; the guardian (*sadin*) of 'Ali's tomb: "The leader has deep connections to this district which carries the tomb of his heroic grandfather (*jaddihi*)," *al-Jumhuriyya*, February 19, 1984.

30. See, for example, Foreign Minister 'Abd al-Karim al-Shaykhali organizing a *Ma'dubat Iftar* (Fast-Breaking Dinner), *al-Jumhuriyya*, Dec. 3, 1968; a party for *Jam'iyyat al-Aadab al-Islamiyya* on *Laylat al-Qadar*, sponsored by the president in Baghdad, whose message was read there and televised, *al-Jumhuriyya*, Dec. 17, 1968 (27 Ramadan); a similar occasion a year later at al-Kaylani's Mosque, fully televised again, *al-Jumhuriyya*, Dec. 6, 1969; very senior officials making speeches on Badr Day, 17 Ramadan, *al-Thawra*, Sept. 2, 1977; the Ministry of Awqaf organizing an *iftar* dinner upon the president's instruction for senior party members, ulama "and citizens" at the tombs of the Shi'i Imams 'Ali al-Hadi [died 254 Hijri] and al-Hasan al-'Askari [died 260 Hijri] in Samarra', *al-Jumhuriyya*, June 25, 1984; and a similar occasion at Kazimayn for party members and "masses," *al-Jumhuriyya*, June 24, 1984; and the party's Branch (*shu'ba*) The Hero of Liberation at *Far'* Saddam Husayn in Saddam City (a Shi'i shanty town in Baghdad) organizing an *iftar* dinner for members, "as part of a series of Ramadan evenings" organized by the party, *al-Thawra*, May 29, 1985.

31. See, for example, "Al-'Ilmaniyya wa Jawhar al-Mawqif al-Ba'thi Min al-Din," in *Al-Thawra al-'Arabiyya*, the internal party organ, disseminated to members only, July 1980, pp. 13–18.

32. For example, *al-Jumhuriyya*, December 6, 1984, a telegram to Saddam Husayn from a celebration of the Prophet's birthday.

33. See, for example, congratulations to the president from the ulama and "men of religion" and visitors to Karbala, *al-Thawra*, February 13, 1988. And a telegram from participants in the celebrations to mark the Prophet's birthday, *al-Jumhuriyya*, December 6, 1984; and ulama in a visit to the battlefront defining Khomeini's regime as "the regime of apostasy from Islam" (*al-nizam al-murtadd*), *al-Qadisiyya*, October 13, 1987; and see *al-Thawra*, January 24, 1988; *al-Jumhuriyya*, December 12, 1987; accusing Tehran of falsifying the Qur'an, *al-Thawra*, June 11, 1981. Deputy Prime Minister Taha Yasin Ramadan to an audience, *al-Thawra*, September 3, 1981.

34. For example, *al-Jumhuriyya*, December 6, 1984; *al-Qadisiyya*, October 3, 1987. See also *al-Thawra*, January 24, 1988.

35. *al-Thawra*, May 19, 1981. For an earlier version see Saddam Husayn in speeches in the Shi'i south soon after Khomeini's return to Tehran, "Islam, a Duty to Save the Nations Via the Arabs" ("al-Islam taklif li inqadh al-umam 'an tariq al-'arab"), *al-Diyar*, 246, February 26, 1979. For Saddam Husayn's source of inspiration see Khayr Allah Tulfah, his maternal uncle, in whose home he grew up, *al-Jumhuriyya*, February 24, 1983. And see ulama in Maysan, *al-Thawra*, July 2, 1981; a cable from a celebration on the eve of the new Islamic year, *al-Thawra*, March 25, 1983; Saddam Husayn's speech

for Christmas, *al-Thawra*, December 25, 1980; ulama to the president, December 12, 1987.

36. For Ramadan see, for example, *al-Jumhuriyya*, November 13, 1968, 21 Sha'ban 1388; *al-Jumhuriyya*, November 5, 1969, 24 Sha'ban 1389; *al-Jumhuriyya*, October 29, 1970, 28 Sha'ban 1390; *al-Jumhuriyya*, October 7, 1972, 28 Sha'ban 1392; *al-Jumhuriyya*, Aug. 12, 1977, 27 Sha'ban 1397; *al-Thawra*, June 30, 1981, 28 Sha'ban 1401; *al-Jumhuriyya*, April 11, 1988, 24 Sha'ban 1408. For Muharram see, for example, *al-Jumhuriyya*, March 19, 1969, 30 Dhu al-Hijja 1388; *al-Jumhuriyya*, March 6, 1970, 28 Dhu al-Hijja 1389; *al-Jumhuriyya*, February 15, 1972, 30 Dhu al-Hijja 1391; *al-Jumhuriyya*, February 2, 1973, 29 Dhu al-Hijja 1392; *al-Jumhuriyya*, January 14, 1975, 1 Muharram 1395.

37. Amendment to the Law of Personal Status, Law No. 21 of 1978, *al-Waqa'i' al-'Iraqiyya*, No. 2639, February 20, 1978.

38. Dr. Mundhir Ibrahim, Minister of Justice, to *al-Thawra*, March 6, 1979.

39. See Law No. 36 of 1972, Eighth Amendment to Law No. 3 of 1931, *WG* 36, Sept. 9, 1972, p. 8; and see amendment to the Penal Code, Law No. 111 of 1968, *WG* 47, November 19, 1980, p. 2, stipulating that the minimum age allowed to enter "taverns" is 18.

40. "Abu Sirhan," *Babil* June 5, 1994, in *FBIS-Serial JN1606153594*. The Law was revoked in 1990 under Western pressure (Ibid.).

41. *Baghdad Voice of the Masses in Arabic*, June 24, 1989, in *FBIS-NES*, June 26, 1989, p. 10.

42. Interview, Tel Aviv, March 29, 1995.

43. *Baghdad Domestic Service in Arabic*, Sept. 5, 1990, in *FBIS-NES*, Sept. 6, 1990, p. 27. In an introduction to the president's speech to soldiers in the Kuwaiti front, *al-Thawra*'s editor wrote of the approaching "scorching confrontation between the Assembly of the [Muslim] Believers (*jam' al-mu'minin*) under Baghdad's leadership, the center of radiation (*markaz al-ish'a*) of Arab civilization and values," and "the assembly of infidels, deviationists and hypocrites led by the U.S." (*al-Thawra*, January 2, 1990); and "the shining center of [Islamic] faith, represented today by great Baghdad," Saddam Husayn Discusses Conditions of Conscripts, *Baghdad Domestic Service in Arabic*, Jan. 2, 1990, in *FBIS-NES*, Jan. 3, 1990, p. 24.

44. *INA in Arabic*, Jan.14, 1991, in *FBIS-NES*, Jan. 14, 1991, p. 38.

45. *NA in Arabic*, April 7, 1991, in *FBIS-NES*, April 8, 1991, p. 33.

46. See an interview with judges and officials from the ministry of interior in *Alif Ba'*, June 8, 1994, pp. 16–19 in *FBIS-Source Line 94LH0077A*. See also,

for example, Mazhar 'Arif's "The Model Official," on corruption in the party, in *Babil*, Nov. 13, 1993, in *JPRS-NEA*, Jan. 13, 1994, p. 6; *Alif Ba'*, June 8, 1994, pp. 16–19, in *FBIS-Source Line 94LH0077A*; an interview with Deputy Prime Minister Taha Yasin Ramadan, admitting that the regime is at a loss in its fight against inflation, by Cairo's *al-Sha'ab*, April 1, 1994, p. 4, in *FBIS-Serial NC0604113294*. For an independent source visiting Baghdad and reporting corruption, "protection" extortion by officials and official thuggery, Peter Waldman, *The Wall Street Journal*, July 21, 1994; and more.

47. *NA in Arabic*, May 29, 1994, in *FBIS-Serial JN2905180994*.

48. Republic of Iraq Radio Network in Arabic, June 4, 1994, in *FBIS-Serial JN0406194294*.

49. Republic of Iraq Radio Network in Arabic, June 5, 1994, in *FBIS-Serial JN0406194294*.

50. *al-Thawra*, August 26, 1990, in *FBIS-Serial JN0109143394*.

51. The Israeli TV, First Network, January 15, 1995, presenting footage from the Iraqi TV, courtesy of CNN.

52. Decree 115 of Aug. 25, 1994, *al-Jumhuriyya*, Sept. 7, 1994, in *FBIS-Serial JN1409142294*; *Reuter* from Baghdad, Sept. 6, 1994.

53. Republic of Iraq Radio Network, July 7, 1994, in *FBIS Serial JN0807075394*.

54. *Al-Qadisiyya*, July 9, 1994, in *FBIS-Serial JN1507094394*.

55. *Babil*, July 19, 1994, in *FBIS-Serial JN1807195194*.

56. See, for example, the internal newsletter for members only *al-Thawra al-'Arabiyya*, Third Year, No. 5–6, 1971, as reproduced in *Al-Fallahun wal-Thawra fi al-Rif* (The Peasants and the Revolution in the Village) (Beirut: Dar al-Tali'a, 1974), pp. 36–45; Dr. Sa'dun Hammadi, the most important social thinker in the Iraqi Ba'th, a few months before the party again came to power in Baghdad, *Qadaya al-Thawra al-'Arabiyya* (Beirut: Dar al-Tali'a lil-Taba'a wal-Nashr, 1968), p. 302; and see Pan-Arab Leadership Member Sa'd Qasim Hammudi, *Afaq 'Arabiyya*, December 1980, p. 94.

57. Saddam Husayn in an Extra-Ordinary Session of the Tenth Regional Congress of the Ba'th party, Republic of Iraq Radio Network in Arabic, October 7, 1992, in *FBIS-NES*, Oct. 8, 1992, pp. 18–19.

58. Some ten interviews with four senior Kurdish activists (one each of the Barazani and Talabani factions, and two independents, one of whom was a son of such a tribal chief-*mustashar*), Washington D.C., January–August 1994; and see for the roles of the Kurdish *mustashars*, many of whom were

tribal chiefs, and their tribal units *afwaj al-difa' al-watani* ("The Battalions of Patriotic Defense"), in the *Anfal* operation, Middle East Watch, *Genocide in Iraq: the Anfal Campaign Against the Kurd* (New York etc.: Human Rights Watch, 1993), pp. 161–166.

59. Hanna Batatu, *The Old Social Classes and the Revolutionary Movements of Iraq* (Princeton: Princeton University Press, 1978), pp. 1027–1028, points out that "the core of the 'Arefite group" consisted of senior army officers belonging to al-Jumayla tribe of the Ramadi province. Also, "many of the men and non-commissioned officers" of 'Abd al-Salam's 'Arif's Twentieth Brigade in 1958, and of his Republican Guard of the mid-1960s, came from the same tribe.

60. Interviews with two Ba'th old-timers who joined the party in 1949 and 1954 respectively, Princeton, September 18, 1994; New York, Sept. 20, 1994. And see, for example, "Alif Ba'al-Ba'th," *al-Ahrar* (Beirut, the organ of the pro-Iraqi faction), March 20, 1970, and reproduced in a booklet of the same name, by Dar al-Tali'a Lil-Taba'a, Beirut, April 1970, pp. 18, 21, 25.

61. See, for example, tribal fighters in Ninneveh describing their exploits, *al-Qadisiyya*, March 16, 1992.

62. For example, interviews with four Shi'i revolutionaries who fled Hilla to Saudi Arabia after the Intifada failed, U.S.A., May 5–8, 1994; and see presidential grants given to Albu 'Aysh and al-'Ama'ira in *nahiyat* al-Fuhud in Dhi Qar for fighting "the bands of traitors" in the *Intifada, al-Thawra,* November 17, 1993. And report that the Bani Hisan, Albu Dish, al-'Isa, al-Shibil, and Saddam Husayn's tribe's Shi'i branch, Albu Nasir of the Najaf area, all supported the regime in the fighting. (*al-Jumhuriyya*, March 19, 1992). That the Bani Hisan supported the regime was confirmed by a Shi'i interviewee from a shaykhly family in Diwaniyya who was one of the leaders of the *Intifada* there (U.S.A., May 6, 1994). The same interviewee, and the four from Hilla, confirmed that the Aal Ribbat near Hilla [possibly the Aal Magsud *fakhdh* within it—author's note] supported the Republican Guard when they re-captured the city.

63. Baghdad Radio, August 30, 1992, in *FBIS-NES*, August 31, 1992.

64. *al-Thawra*, August 1, 1993. For officials visiting the tribal *mudif* see, for example, the visit by the secretary of the Basra branch (*far'*) of the party to the *mudif* of Shaykh 'Abd al-Rasul Khudayr of the Bani Ka'b tribe near Basra, *al-Thawra*, Oct. 7, 1992; the Zubayd, Jubbur al-Luhayb, al-Hurub, Bani Zayd, and the Sadah in a nahiya in Diyala, inviting to a meeting the secretary of the Central Tanzim of the party, Muhammad Yunis al-Ahmad and swearing allegiance, *al-Thawra*, Oct. 5, 1992; the Jubbur tribes thanking the president for sending his representative to deliver his condolences

upon the death of Ahmad al-Humud al-'Abd Rabbo of Ninneveh, Shaykh al-Masha'ikh of all the Jubburs, *al-Thawra*, Oct. 9, 1992.

65. *Lajnat al-ta'bi'a al-sha'biyya lil-difa' 'an al-'iraq al-'azim . . ., al-Jumhuriyya*, March 4, 1992.

66. See, for example, tribal chiefs meeting in Kazimiyya, the old Shi'i quarter, *al-Thawra*, August 16, 1992.

67. Saddam Husayn is publicly connected with the Beygat, *al-Thawra*, July 17, 1993; and *al-Thawra*, January 25, 1993. On the president's and other luminaries' affiliation to Aal Nasir, see Yunis Ibrahim al-Samarra'i, *Al-Qaba'il al-'Iraqiyya* (Baghdad: Maktabat al-Sharq al-Jadid, 1989), Vol. 2, pp. 655–658; and many others.

68. See, for example, Nuri Khalil al-Barazi, *Al-Badu Wal-Istiqrar Fi al-'Iraq* (Cairo: Ma'had al-Buhuth wal-Dirasat al-'Arabiyya, the Arab League, 1969).

69. For example, Humud Hammadi al-Sa'idi, *'An 'Asha'ir al-'Iraq* (Baghdad: Maktabat al-Nahda, 1988); Yunis al-Shaykh Ibrahim al-Samarra'i, *Al-Qaba'il Wal-Buyutat al-Hashimiyya fi al-'Iraq* (Baghdad: Maktabat al-Sharq al-Jadid, 1988); ibid., *Al-Qaba'il al-'Iraqiyya* (Baghdad: Maktabat al-Sharq al-Jadid, 1989), Vols. I, II; Al-Hajj 'Abd al-Hasan al-Mufaw'ar al-Sudani, *Al-'Adat Wal-Taqalid al-'Asha'iriyya fi al-'Amara* (Baghdad: Matba'at al-Jahiz, 1990). And in the popular press see, for example, *al-Thawra*, August 16, 1992, an interview with 'Abd al-Hasan al-Mufaw'ar, defined as an expert on tribal folklore; and see a symposium in the Mustansiriyya University on the political role of tribes between the two world wars, *al-Thawra*, Dec. 28, 1992.

70. *al-Thawra*, December 3, 1992.

71. Thus, for example, the editor of the government daily explained Iraq's decision to stay in Kuwait despite the UN Coalition's military advantage in terms of "Tribal honor" (*al-sharaf al-'asha'iri*). Salah Mukhtar, *al-Jumhuriyya*, January 5, 1994.

72. See, for example, Dia' Hasan, "Who are the Iraqis," *al-Thawra*, Oct. 22, 1992.

73. Jabbar 'Abd Allah al-Jawibrawi, author of *'Asha'ir al-Furat al-Awsat wal-Janub* (Baghdad, 1992), and *Ta'rikh Maysan wa 'Asha'ir al-'Amara* (Baghdad, 1990). See *al-Thawra*, Sept. 7, 1992.

74. *Babil*, December 6, 1993.

75. *Babil*, November 1, 1993.

76. *Babil*, October 21, 1992, in *FBIS-Serial JN2310103594*. And see, for exam-

ple, a complaint that the Haditha police are unable to stop such disputes, *Babil*, October 17, 1993.

77. *al-Qadisiyya*, January 10, 1994.

78. Washington, D.C., January 25, 1993.

The Appeal of Conspiracy Theories to Persians

AHMAD ASHRAF

Although conspiracy paradigms are found in belief systems through-out the world, they seem to have been more prevalent in the Middle East, particularly among Persians, than in other societies.[1] The appeal of con-spiracy theories to Persians arises from a combination of factors such as the legacy of deep rooted pre-Islamic and Shi'ite cultural beliefs about satanic forces; frequent foreign interference during the period of semi-colonialism in the 19th and early 20th centuries and the great power pol-itics of the 1940s–80s; the autocratic, non-participatory style of Persian politics combined with tight control of the press and media; as well as the effectiveness of conspiracy theories as a collective defense mechanism, particularly during periods of powerlessness, defeat, and political tur-moil.[2]

In conspiracy theories, one or more groups—national, ethnic, inter-national, religious, political, or commercial—are believed to plot secret-ly against other groups, primarily the theorist's own. Revolutions, defeats, underdevelopment, and other failures and disasters are thus blamed on powerful external enemies and their domestic agents. Conspiracy theories can often be reduced to a Manichean world-view in which the world is divided between good and evil powers with satanic forces directing the course of history. The agents of conspiracy theories, real or imaginary, are conceived as the real enemy, as the main evil, as satanic forces of darkness who are powerful, well organized, but masked, invisible, sinister, and dehumanized figures. Blaming others for one's own failure often serves an important social function; it helps assuage the anxiety of the group members at times of stress. It allows one to reduce complexity in stress situations. Current research in social psychology sees conspiracy theories as a mode of causal attribution and, like scientific theories, logically coherent. Elaborate and internally consistent systems of thought that are maintained for emotional reasons, conspiracy theories are held tenaciously and are extremely difficult to refute.[3]

Beginning with a brief examination of the cultural, political, and social psychological context of conspiracy theories among Persians this article will discuss the two general types of conspiracy theories prevalent in modern Persia: those dealing with more particularistic plots by Western colonial powers, Great Britain, Russia, and the United States; and those dealing with more universalistic satanic forces acting against Persia from antiquity to the present. The article will also elaborate on recent attempts at unmasking conspiracy theories held by Persians.

Why Conspiracy Theories?

Iranian mythology from antiquity includes stories about conspiratorial schemes against Persia's legendary or heroic figures from the very time of its foundation. Created in the center of the universe, Iran encountered conspiracies from the West (the Greco-Roman world) and the East (Turco-Chinese peoples). Iraj, the first king of Persia, was the victim of jealousy and conspiracy of his brothers Sam and Tour, the kings of the West and the East, who murdered him and sent his head to their father Faridun. The Western schemes culminated in Alexander's conquest of Persia, who, following Aristotle's advice, dismantled the empire and the central institution of the kingship and divided Iran into numerous decentralized small kingdoms in order to ensure the stability and prosperity of the West.[4] The fear of Satanic forces remained alive among Persians in the Islamic era and, more specifically, in the Shi'ite conception of the world. The Shi'ite view of the Imams as victims of conspiracies of the caliphs, the sharp distinction between the exoteric (*zaher*) and the esoteric (*baten*), a tradition of attributing miraculous deeds to the twelve Imams, and the practice of the prudential dissimulation of belief (*taqiya*) were all conducive to the conspiratorial world-view.[5] Furthermore, a receptivity to the mythological mode of thought, the mythological character of traditional Persian historiography, and the proclivity of all Persians, notables as well as commoners, toward poetic exaggeration (*eghraq-e sha'erana*) in describing the world, have all contributed to the popularity of conspiracy theories among them.

A transition from metaphysical to worldly conspiracy theories during modern times has led to a deeper belief that satanic forces are at work in the lives of Persians. In the 20th century, when the social paradigm changed and a cognitive reorientation took place in the social imagination of Persians, novel theories were developed to explain the causes of Persia's decline in modern times. Whereas in Europe the French Revolution marked a new era in the burgeoning of a variety of worldly conspiracy theories, it was the Constitutional Revolution that led to the prevalence of these theories in Persia.

The apparent absence of worldly conspiracy theories in 19th-century Persia, and their swift rise and increasing popularity in the 20th century, make it likely that such theories emerged to a great extent as a result of the weakness of central authority and the rise of foreign interventions in the country's internal affairs in a semi-colonial situation. The formation of worldly conspiracy theories in the course of the Constitutional Revolution of 1905–1909 and its aftermath seems to have been influenced by the anti-Russian and pro-British posture of the Revolution, Persia's division into zones of British and Russian influence in 1907, and the occupation of the country during World War I by the British, Russian, and Ottoman-German forces, the semi-protectorate agreement with Britain in 1919, and the British-backed coup d'état of 1921 that led to the establishment of the Pahlavi dynasty. During most of this period, foreign embassies both openly and covertly intervened through and by individual political notables, tribal khans, big merchants, and ulama.[6] Thus, many members of the country's political elites became agents of the Western powers and used foreign patronage to enhance their political power. As Peter Avery has noted, for Persian notables

> Foreign patronage was found extremely tempting: it was easy to overcome rivals and to mislead timid compatriots with the air of being 'in the know', knowing what the British or Russians wanted and being able to hint darkly at the consequences of their wants going unsatisfied. The scope foreign contracts afforded local intrigues was an important feature of Iran's entanglement with the Great Powers.[7]

These notables, hinting at knowledge of the real intentions of the foreigners, contributed to a general sense that Persian affairs were directed by hidden plotters in foreign embassies. Moreover, rival embassies and their clients fabricated and disseminated numerous conspiratorial tales to discredit their enemies. At the same time, students returning from the West imported German and French anti-British conspiracy theories to Persia. All these factors helped the formation and popularity of conspiracy theories during this period.

The popularity of conspiracy theories in Persia can also be traced to their function as a collective defense mechanism. Blame-placing schemata often serve an important social-psychological function: they allow one to ignore the complex causes of a breakdown of the social world and hence help groups under stress to feel relieved of responsibility for their situations. For the proud Persians, who are ever conscious of their long history and also consider their country to have been created in the center of the universe, the debacles of defeat and loss of territory in modern times have created a crisis of identity and collective consciousness which in turn have persuaded them to search not only for explanations, but also for relief and reassurance.

Furthermore, the authoritarian, non-participatory style of Persian politics, the weakness of civil society vis-á-vis the sprawling petrolic state apparatus, combined with the tight control of the press and media and suppression of free expression of ideas, are all conducive to a general feeling of insecurity, suspicion of state policies and strategies, and mistrust of the news disseminated by the government-controlled media. These conditions have largely influenced the proliferation of political gossip and conspiracy theories among the political elite as well as the middle and lower classes.

A telling example of the positive effects of free debate and discussion in unraveling conspiracy theories is the partial rehabilitation of Reza Shah, even among a group of radical Islamists, in the post-revolutionary period when it became possible to present new facts and analysis about a man who was the target of a greater variety of conspiracy theories than any other statesman in the modern history of Iran. A key accusation against Reza Shah has been his dramatic decision in 1932 to toss the file of d'Arcy's oil concession into the fireplace. He later signed the new Anglo-Persian Oil Agreement which extended the term of the old agreement for 32 more years and had it ratified by the Majlis. The popular theory has been that since the original concession was granted by Mozaffar al-Din Shah in the pre-Constitutional period, the British strongly desired to have it extended and approved by the Majlis in order to endow it with legal stature. Thus, this "show" is widely considered as the final act of the pre-planned British scheme for the rise of Reza Shah to power and the formation of the Pahlavi dynasty.

A new interpretation of this event that was published in the post-revolutionary period indicates that Reza Shah, unaware of international implications of cancelling the oil agreement, believed that he was dealing only with the British oil company and not with the British government. Furthermore, the Shah agreed to extend the terms of the concession—as demanded by the British in the last days of the negotiations—apparently because of excessive British pressure and the province of Khuzestan's threat to secede from Iran. Mojtaba Minovi, an eminent Persian scholar, encouraged Sayyed Hasan Taqizada to tell the story of these events and transcribed Taqizada's account. According to one source, the transcription was stolen from Minovi's study room by SAVAK agents in the late 1950s after he disclosed its existence to a friend who leaked the news to the security agency.[8] The Pahlavi regime chose to suppress the historical facts and continue the usual glorification of Reza Shah as an infallible leader. Had it permitted the exposure of the facts about the incident and a free public analysis regarding the facts, Reza Shah would have emerged as a patriot concerned with Iranian national interest, albeit oblivious to the realities of international power politics. Clearly, the regime's choice perpetuated conspiratorial interpretations of the whole episode.

Particularistic Conspiracy Theories

Although there are Persian conspiracy theories implicating all the Western powers competing in Persia, including Russia, Great Britain, Germany, and the United States, those involving the British have been the most popular among members of the elite and the middle classes born before World War II. In this section, conspiracy theories involving Britain, Russia and the United States will be discussed.

1. The British Conspiratorial Schema

Many Persians believe that the British have controlled the course of modern world history, including all the major historical events in Persia from the Russo-Persian wars of the early 19th century to the revolution of February 1979. According to this theory, the cold-blooded, foxy, and cunning British (*rubah-e makkar*), who could "cut off the heads of their enemies even with cotton"—that is, who possessed nearly miraculous powers to achieve their ends smoothly—duped and manipulated the "simple Russians" and the "naive Yankees." The anti-British theories were influenced by conspiracy theories created in France and Germany beginning in the 18th century and imported to Persia by returning students in the early 20th century.[9] Moreover, the anti-British propaganda of the Russians, Germans, and Ottomans in the late 19th and early 20th centuries increased fears of a secret British design against Persia and the Islamic world.[10]

British influence in Persia began in the early 19th century and grew rapidly after the Constitutional Revolution of 1905–11, lasting (except in the 1930s) until the oil nationalization movement of 1951–53. British influence was increased by the Persian belief in the *siasat-e Engelis*, the almost magical power of the British to manipulate virtually everything in Persia and throughout the world. It was believed that most political events were stage-managed by the British and that almost all politicians were British agents. Anything could be the work of the British, and any person could be their agent.[11] The assassination, execution, or murder of political leaders was also attributed to the hidden hand of the British.[12] In this drama of conspiracy, a significant role is played by the popular figures (*wajih al-mella*) who pretend to oppose British interests (*na'l-e varuna zadan*, lit. "put their horse's shoes on backwards"). Thus, for example, even though the leaders of the pro-German, anti-British Iranian Nationalist Committee (Komita-ye Melliyun-e Irani), founded in Berlin in 1915, the communist Tudeh Party in the 1940s, the Oil Nationalization Movement of 1950–53, and the 1979 Revolution acted overtly and vigorously against British interests in Persia, it was believed that they were actually directed by the British grandmaster in the "puppet show of politics."[13]

The myth of *siyasat-e Engelis* was applied retroactively to the 19th century, when Russia was the still dominant foreign power in Persia. For example, in his influential book *The Hidden Hand of British Policy in Iran*, Ahmad Khan Malek Sasani, an ardent anti-British conspiracy theorist, lays out a great British conspiracy to dismantle Persia.[14] The massacre of the Russian minister in Tehran (Alexander Gribaedov) and his staff by a mob on 11 February 1829 was intended to encourage Russia to annex the Caucasus and make further advances into Persia.[15] The British induced the Ottomans to occupy Bahrain, the Turkomans Gorgan, and the Afghans Sistan.[16] They had the grand vizier Abu'l-Qasem Qa'em-Maqam murdered because he championed Persia's geographical integrity.[17] Khan Malek Sasani describes how British diplomats told some Jews that Mirza Taqi Khan Amir Kabir was plotting to usurp the throne. When this rumor reached Naser al-Din Shah, he dismissed the Amir and subsequently ordered his execution.[18] Khan Malek Sasani also asserts that British agents tricked the Russians into taking such outrageous measures as bombarding the shrine of the eighth Imam in Mashhad in 1912 in order to foster Persian hatred of Russians.[19] According to Khan Malek Sasani the British also meddled in religious matters. They controlled the ulama through the so-called "Indian money," money donated by Shi'ites in British India and transferred to the ulama in Iraq through British diplomatic channels.[20] The British also encouraged the Babis to rebel in the mid-19th century, instigated pogroms against the Baha'is to force them to collaborate with British agents in return for protection, and encouraged Jews to become Baha'is in order to allow them to forge closer ties with the families of Persian notables and spy on them.[21]

Khan Malek Sasani's theories culminate in his account of British treatment of Persian notables. The British, he charges, punished those notables who had opposed their policies. The punishment included defamation, dismissal from office, imprisonment, and assassination for the notables themselves, and political obscurity for their families. Khan Malek Sasani claims that, according to the statistics at his disposal, about twenty old notable families who were British agents, aided by eighty second-level old and new families, ruled Persia from the mid-19th to the mid-20th century.

> The descendants of the dirty dozen who collaborated with Colonel Sheil (the British Minister in Tehran) in murdering Amir Kabir, still, after a century, hold key positions. Any family whose members have occupied key positions in the last hundred years with no interruption are all the servants of Great Britain.[22]

Mahmud Mahmud, a more serious historian, has produced a detailed study of the British scheme for Persia in his well-received and influential eight-volume "A History of Anglo-Persian Political Relations in the 19th Century." Mahmud believes that the Qajars were under Russian protection and British influence for over a century. The Tobacco Rebellion of 1890–91 dealt a blow to British influence in Persia. However, the British learned a lesson and began to appreciate the significance of the ulama in mob mobilization. They used the "Indian money," which was put at the disposal of the British envoy in Baghdad, to infiltrate the high-ranking ulama in the Shi'ite holy cities of southern Iraq.[23] The British instigated a group of the ulama to demand a constitutional regime in 1905–1907. The Constitutional Revolution, according to Mahmud, led to the weakening of the state and the rise to power of the "vile lower classes." The main British objective in stage-managing the Constitutional Revolution was to dominate Persia through the 1907 Treaty, which divided Persia into two zones of influence and a neutral zone in between.

> The British murdered the great and powerful Naser al-Din Shah to replace him with the ailing Mozaffar al-Din Shah. They removed Muhammad-'Ali Shah to bring to the Peacock throne the ailing boy, Ahmad Shah.[24]

The fall of the Qajars and the rise of the Pahlavis is a favorite topic of the conspiracy theories. Some conspiracy theorists believe that the British plotted to overthrow the Qajars from the time the Russians established the succession of Qajar monarchs in the descendants of the Crown Prince 'Abbas Mirza as part of the Torkomanchay Treaty in 1828.[25] Though Reza Khan had actually attempted a coup with German aid as early as 1917, the British did play a major role in the 22 February 1921 coup d'état that actually brought him to power.[26] This undisputed fact has grown into a mythology in which every event and every action by Reza Khan (later Reza Shah) was controlled by the British. Thus, General Ironside presumably selected from the outset an "illiterate, crude soldier" (Reza Khan) to carry out the plot.[27] The next step in the British design was to force Ahmad Shah to abdicate, a design which is often attributed to the latter's refusal to support the 1919 Anglo-Persian semi-protectorate agreement.[28]

It was firmly believed that "the British raised Reza Shah to glory and threw him out when he became useless." Thus, it is widely believed that Reza Shah was commissioned by British intelligence to implement its scheme for Persia, including the construction of the trans-Persian railway, which is said to have been designed in advance by the British for use during World War II.

The murder of 'Abd al-Hosayn Teymurtash and Nosrat-al-Dawla Firuz under the police custody and the suicide of 'Ali-Akbar Davar in the 1930s are also attributed to the British design. The unveiling of women, the attempt to purify Persian from Arabic loan-words, the uncovering of plots against the life of Reza Shah, and even the establishment of the National Bank and the issuing of paper currency, were parts of a British design to contaminate Persian culture, foment Arab-Persian conflict, control the Shah, and plunder Persia's gold and silver.[29]

The British were also said to have established the Qom theological center in the early 1920s with the secret support of Reza Khan as part of a scheme to contain communist encroachment in Persia.[30] On the other hand, many members of the ulama believe that it was the British who were behind Reza Khan's policy of suppressing the ulama at Qom and other religious centers.[31]

The granting of oil concessions to the British and the activities of the

British Petroleum Company have been the subject of elaborate conspiracy theories since the turn of the century. A story made up by French and Austrian journalists explaining how the British government was able to steal the 1319/1901 oil concession from William Knox d'Arcy was widely believed by Persians.[32] Another oil-related British conspiratorial design was seen in the rumors of a miraculous fountain (*Saqqa Khana-ye Shaikh Hadi*) in Tehran in July 1924. The site attracted thousands of superstitious people, a situation that ended in the murder of the American consul, Robert Imbrie, who was "persuaded by the hidden hand of the British to make an appearance and take pictures." Many Persians believed that the British objective was to scare off the Sinclair Oil Company that was in the process of acquiring oil concessions in northern Persia, whereas the informed sources believed that it was Reza Khan who took advantage of the incident to establish his firm military control over the country.[33] Other prevalent conspiracy theories maintain that Reza Shah's cancellation of the D'Arcy concession and conclusion of a new oil agreement in 1933, which extended the concession to 1992 (for thirty-two more years), was a preplanned British design.[34]

The myth of *siyasat-e Engelis* surfaced once again during the Allied occupation of Persia in 1941 and its aftermath. The ascension to the throne of the crown prince Muhammad Reza, the selection of cabinets, the results of Majles elections, the rise and fall of personalities, political parties, social clubs, and newspapers, and even famines and food shortages were all attributed to British scheming.[35] Another conspiracy theory holds that the pro-Soviet Tudeh Party was formed by British agents and served the interests of the British Petroleum Company. This theory, introduced by those who split from the party in the mid-1940s, became prevalent among nationalist groups. The basis for this accusation was that Mostafa Fateh, a director of the petroleum company, was instrumental in creating the Anti-Fascist United Front in cooperation with VOX (the Soviet cultural center). Several founding members of the Tudeh Party were active in VOX; and some, including Bozorg 'Alawi and Ehsan Tabari, found well-paid jobs in Victory House (the British cultural center) and the British Petroleum Company. This cooperation, though simply a wartime tactical move, was interpreted as the secret hand of the British operating in the Tudeh Party.[36] Some even believed in a secret

Anglo-Russian scheme against Persia. General Hajj 'Ali Razmara, for example, was accused of being involved in a plot to establish a British-led pro-Soviet regime in Persia.[37]

In another class of theories the imaginary formation of a mysterious religious organization, the Islamic Jehad Party (Hezb-e Jehad-e Islami), in the early 1940s was attributed to the British. The party was said to have directed the activities of the Shi'ite ulama in Qom and Najaf as well as the operations of the Tudeh party and leftist guerrilla groups such as Feda'ian-e Khalq and Mojahedin-e Khalq.[38] The court minister and former premier 'Abd al-Hosayn Hazhir and Prime Minister Hajj 'Ali Razmara were assassinated in 1949 and 1951 by Feda'ian-e Islam, a militant underground organization that was believed by many to be, like the Muslim Brethren of Egypt, a British creation.[39]

Even the shahs were influenced by such theories. Reza Shah believed that "the British were behind all evils of the world . . . . he even suspected his son [the crown prince Muhammad Reza] of being a British agent."[40] Amir Asad Allah Alam, Muhammad Reza Shah's close confidant and court minister, relates that the Shah's

> Suspicions of the British are quite incredible; he tends to see their secret hand behind virtually every international incident. For myself I'm confident that they're more or less incapable of achieving anything on the international stage, to such an extent that their power declined.[41]

Muhammad Reza Shah believed that the assassination attempts against his life in 1950 and 1966 were Anglo-Soviet designs.[42] He believed, for example, that Iraq's President "Hasan al-Bakr may pose as an anglophobe but in reality he's a lackey of the British."[43] Muhammad Reza Shah even suspected the anglophobic Mosaddeq of being a British agent:

> We always suspected he was a British agent, a suspicion his future posturing as an anti-British nationalist did not diminish. Certainly my father had long suspected his British connections and in 1940 jailed him on espionage charges.[44]

The shah believed that "Mosaddeq's negative nationalism, paradoxically, allowed the British more influence over Persia's national policies than ever before."[45]

At the time of the 1979 revolution the notion of a British anti-Persian conspiracy reappeared. The anti-American posture of the revolution and the BBC's regular broadcasting of the daily news of the revolution left no doubts for the Shah and for many older upper- and middle-class Persians that British agents had stage-managed the revolution.[46] Thus, for example, Princess Ashraf relates that "These riots took place during a steady campaign of biased anti-Shah news reports by the BBC, almost a reprise of the attacks made on my father few decades earlier."[47]

The fact that revolutionary mobilization further advanced during the premiership of Ja'far Sharifemami, the grand master of the Persian national freemasonry lodge, further confirmed suspicions of a British conspiracy.[48] The old suspicion that "the ulama had a historical connection with Indian money and with the British" also led many members of the elite and the old-guard politicians to believe that even the anti-Western Imam Khomeini was a British agent.[49] Thus, for example, the shah told the British ambassador that "if you lift up Khomeini's beard, you will find "Made in England" written under his chin."[50] Some theorists further explain that the revolution was instigated by the British to eliminate the shah because he had placed himself at the disposal of the Americans.[51] Some conspiracy theorists also believe that the main conspirator in the Revolution was the multinational Oil Consortium, which allegedly was dominated by British interests.[52] Conspiracy theorists accusing the British found some of their views confirmed in such publications as the *Executive Intelligence Review*, sponsored by Lyndon LaRouche and his disciples, which argued that President Jimmy Carter, Zbigniew Brzezinski, Henry Kissinger, Ramsey Clark, and Cyrus Vance, among others, served as the "British fifth column" and helped bring about the Islamic Revolution, "a carefully orchestrated British Military Intelligence operation."[53]

2. The Testament of Peter the Great

The Testament of Peter the Great was fabricated in 1795 by Polish anti-Russian emigrants in Paris who sought to arouse the French public against Russia.[54] Belief in the authenticity of the *Testament* was widespread among anti-Russian Persians.[55] According to the *Testament* the Russians had developed a secret design with two major objectives: to subjugate Europe and to conquer Persia and thereby reach the warm southern waters. The Russian Revolution of 1917 and Lenin's 1921 treaty with Persia tempered Persian Russophobia for a while, but it revived with Stalin's abortive attempt to annex Azerbaijan in 1945. In the early 1950s, the CIA disseminated a forged memoir attributed to Abu'l-Qasem Lahuti, a poet and noted revolutionary leader who had lived in the Soviet Union since his abortive rebellion in Azerbaijan in 1922. The author of the forgery, an American Iranist and CIA consultant, believed that Lahuti was a natural candidate for the premiership of Soviet-dominated Persia. The memoirs indicated, among other things, that the Russians planned to annex all of the northern provinces of Persia.[56] Thus, in the words of Muhammad Reza Shah, "Ever since Peter the Great, who ruled from 1682 to 1725, Russia had in fact been trying to expand southward to obtain warm-water ports on the Persian Gulf."[57]

Interest in *The Testament of Peter the Great* was revived once again in the late 1970s and early 1980s. Many old guard politicians and members of the middle class saw the Islamic Revolution, the Soviet invasion of Afghanistan, and the occupation of the American embassy as examples of the hidden hand of the Soviets seeking to fulfill *The Testament of Peter the Great*.[58] Many believed the rumor that Muhammad Musawi Kho'iniha, the militant clergyman who directed the hostage crisis, was one of dozens of Russian agents who had infiltrated Qom, and that the "liberal-nationalist-Islamic" triad of Abu'l Hasan Bani Sadr, Ebrahim Yazdi, and Sadeq Qotbzada were militant Marxists who had infiltrated and dominated Ayatollah Khomeini's group.[59]

The idea of a secret British-Russian design has been popular since the 1907 agreement between the two countries that divided Persia into two zones of influence.[60] General Hosayn Fardust, among others, believes that the "British and Russians are cooperating in fomenting this crisis."

Commenting on Fardust's theory, Ambassador William Sullivan says that "we often hear this fantastic charge."[61] Thus, for example, the hostage crisis of 1979–81 is seen as a repetition of the Imbrie affair of 1924 in which the Russians and the British supposedly acted in concert against

American interests in Persia.[62] The exiled shah attributed the events in Persia to the "Unholy Alliance of Red and Black [i.e., the Left and the British agents, the clerics]."[63]

3. The Central Intelligence Agency

After the Central Intelligence Agency (CIA) engineered the 1953 coup that overthrew the Mosaddeq government, the dominant position of the United States in Persia began to be reflected in the conspiracy theories held by many Persians.[64] The Persian elite of the post-Mosaddeq period, an American diplomat noted, believed in the myth of "American omnipotence." Imagining that in reality prime ministers were chosen by the U.S., he relates, "Candidates or would-be candidates for prime minister come to advertise their assets and their availability."[65] It was widely believed that the White Revolution and the land reform program of the 1960s were designed in detail by the Americans, though in fact U.S. officials had favored a more moderate land reform.[66] The leftists and many in the middle class believed that these reforms were designed by the Americans to undermine the feudal bases of British interests in Persia.[67] Khomeini, among others, saw the land reform as a U.S. plot to destroy Persian agriculture in order to create a market for surplus American produce and to make Persia dependent upon the U.S. for her food supply.[68] Opponents of the shah blamed many internal events on SAVAK and the security forces acting as agents of the CIA and the United States. Tens of thousands of people were rumored to have been tortured and executed by drowning in the salt lake in southern Tehran. The deaths of such figures as Gholam-Reza Takhti (1967), Jalal Al-e Ahmad (1968), Hasan Arsanjani (1969), 'Ali Shari'ati (1975), and Sayyed Mostafa Khomeini (1977) were rumored to be secret murders officially disguised as suicide, heart attacks, and strokes.[69]

The most important conspiracy theory involving the U.S. is the belief that the Persian Revolution of February 1979 was masterminded by the Carter administration either to create a barrier to the southward movement of the Soviet Union or to prevent Persia from becoming a major power. Many royalists adduce two major pieces of "hard evidence" for this theory: General Robert Huyser's secret mission to Persia and the

Guadeloupe summit on 14 January 1979 in which the West supposedly decided to replace the shah with an Islamic regime. The shah wrote:

> I believe that during these meetings the French and the West Germans agreed with the British and the American proposals to my ouster. These Guadeloupe meetings may prove to be the 'Yalta of the Mideast,' with the notable absence of the recipient (U.S.S.R.) of the largesse . . . . 'General Huyser threw the shah out of the country like a dead mouse.'[70]

Some leftists even see the occupation of the American embassy in Tehran in 1979–80 as providing a pretext for the Carter administration to freeze $14 billion in Persian assets in the United States. According to the shah the events in Persia and Afghanistan indicated a grand Russian and American conspiracy by which they "have divided the world between them."[71]

The Persian Left has developed its own conspiracy theories concerning the United States. In general, the U.S. intends to keep the Third World in a state of dependency. In Persia the capitalist West and its internal agents, the dependent bourgeoisie, are behind various plots, coups, regional wars, and so forth.[72] The Left saw the White Revolution and land reform of the 1960s as a U.S. scheme to encourage further development of dependent capitalism, the decline of the agricultural sector, and mass migration to the cities.[73] Some see the Islamic Revolution and hostage-taking as a conspiracy between Khomeini and Reagan to bring about Carter's electoral defeat.[74] The Iran-Contra affair is believed to have substantiated this theory. Many leftists believe that the West, led by U.S. imperialism, allowed Khomeini's group to hijack the revolution in order to repress the revolutionary Left and to keep Persia under Western influence.[75] Persian Maoists believe in a U.S.-Soviet conspiracy. Some even believe that all the policies of the Islamic Republic have been orchestrated by the United States and Great Britain in order to safeguard the interests of the world capitalist system.[76]

Calling the U.S. the "great Satan" and blaming it for the creation of an emasculated version of Islam (Eslam-e Amrika'i), Ayatollah Khomeini and the radical elements within the Islamic regime consider the U.S. as the great world conspirator, engaged in an ongoing plot against Persia and

Islam.[77] In contrast, Abu'l-Hasan Bani-Sadr, the ousted president of the Islamic Republic, is an ardent proponent of a "Reagan-Khomeini" conspiracy theory. He points to numerous secret relations between the U.S. and the leaders of the Islamic regime and believes that the regime is a U.S. puppet.[78]

Universalistic Conspiracy Theories

The satanic historical conspiracy theories claim that inimical global forces conspiring to prevent Persia from attaining its natural position of political, military, cultural, or religious superiority. The satanic conspirators include Hellenic Westernism, Freemasonry, Zionism, the Baha'i religion, and even the Shi'ite clergy.

1. Hellenic Westernism

The uneasy relationship between Persia and the Western powers from antiquity to the present has encouraged intellectuals like Ahmad Fardid, Zabih Behruz, and Hosayn Malek to adopt theories of conspiracy. The term *gharbzadagi* (literally "plagued by the West" or "West-toxication") was coined by Fardid, who claimed that the Freemasons and Jews were engaged in a great conspiracy to Hellenize the world, including the West.[79] The concept of West-toxication appears to follow from the notion of the "darkening of the world," a recurring theme in Martin Heidegger's works. The decadence of the West, says Fardid, had already begun in the Hellenic philosophy with the human being's (*wojud*) loss of oneness with consciousness (*delagahi*). Western man, immersed in technology, is more concerned with his being than with his spiritual calling in the world. Humanism, the idea that man is at the center of universe and replaces God, has been the ethos of the West since the time of the Hellenic philosophers. This humanist ethos is in conflict, says Fardid, with the spiritual ethos of the Orient. But the Orient has lost its cultural potency and is dominated by Western civilization. The liberal conception of the free society is useless in a world in which being (*wojud*) and consciousness (*delagahi*) are no longer well integrated; Fardid believes that the

Constitutional Revolution in particular was tainted by the West through Freemasonry and Judaism. Fardid's theories have been used by some intellectuals to claim that the policies of the Islamic regime were a form of Oriental spiritualism.[80]

Behruz has argued that the Persian nation has been the victim of a conspiracy perpetrated by the Western world from antiquity to the present whose purpose has been to prevent Persia from assuming its natural role as the world's most powerful nation. This Western conspiracy was responsible for spreading the false notion that Alexander the Great actually conquered Persia.[81] Behruz holds that clandestine Manichean societies, disguised under various names, have proved to be the most vicious and destructive conspiratorial force in history; they had been responsible, among other things, for the defeat of Persia by the Arabs in the 7th century and the conquest of Persia by the Mongols in the 13th century, as well as for all rebellious movements in the medieval Islamic Persia. The main secret device used by Manichean conspirators had been the frequent distortion of every calendar system to confuse and divert the course of history.[82]

In *Tawallod-e Ghulha* (The birth of ogres) Malek has elaborated on the notions of Fardid and Behruz, arguing that the Western conspiracy was initiated when Persia—with a superior culture and civilization that contrasted fundamentally with those of the Hellenes—defeated Greece in the Peloponnesian wars of the 6th century B.C.E. In retaliation for that defeat the West has ceaselessly opposed Persia.[83] Malek believes that during this struggle, Judaism, which has dominated the Hellenic West, became the great conspirator and provided the West with five poisonous gifts: Christianity from Jesus, communism from Marx, psychoanalysis from Freud, the atomic bomb from Einstein, and the Club of Rome from Herman Kahn.[84] One example of Western satanic conspiracies is the superimposition of the alien Hellenic notions of "law" and "democracy" on the Persian world through the Constitutional Revolution.[85]

2. The Crusaders' Conspiracy Against Islam.

Many Muslim intellectuals in Persia—notably Khomeini, Mortaza Motahhari, Jalal Al-e Ahmad, and 'Ali Shari'ati—believe in a general conspiracy of the Christian West to prevent the rise of Islam and its van-guard nation, Shi'ite Persia. They believe that since the Crusades the West has plotted to subjugate the Islamic world and inhibit its prosperity and development. More specifically, they believe that there was a Western conspiracy to dissolve the Ottoman Empire, foment internal conflict among Muslim communities, support Israel and world Zionism, and brainwash the younger generation of Muslims. Thus, Khomeini believed that Salman Rushdie's *Satanic Verses* was part of the conspiracy of the Christian West to humiliate the Muslim world.[86] Another variant sees the rise of the Shi'ite Safavid empire as a conspiracy of the Christian West to split the Muslim world and undermine the true Islam of Shi'ism.[87]

3. Conspiracy of the Shi'ite Ulama

Shoja' al-Din Shafa, a former Persian deputy court minister for cul-tural affairs, developed another grand conspiracy theory based on ideas found in the shah's last book—that is, that a "strange amalgam"—the Shi'ite clergy, the leftists, the Western media, the major oil companies, and the British and American governments—was formed to destroy the rapidly developing Persia.[88] Shafa suggests that "The emergence of the Shi'ite ulama in the 10th century constitutes the greatest conspiracy in Persian history and perhaps the oldest conspiracy in world history."[89] The purpose was to emasculate the anti-establishment potential of true Shi'ism by transforming it into the instrument of corrupt Shi'ite leaders. Three "capital investments" ensured the loyalty of the ulama. First, the ulama acquired the financial support of the temporal authorities and the *bazaris*—a "secret coalition" of the forces of tyranny (*estebdad*), exploita-tion (*estef'mar*), and demagoguery (*estehmar*).[90] The second "capital investment" in the ulama came from Great Britain in the late 19th centu-ry, using the "Indian money" and other contributions.[91] The third was made in the 1970s by a multinational consortium of the big oil compa-nies, the CIA, British Intelligence, the KGB, and Mossad.[92] This gigantic satanic coalition, using the ulama to mobilize the Islamic Revolution in Persia, was able to stop the development of Persia and prevent its impending entry into the "Northern Club."[93]

4. Conspiracies of the Freemasons, Baha'is, and Zionists

The belief in a joint conspiracy of Freemasonry, the Baha'i, and Zionism have been the most widely accepted in Persia, particularly in religious and nationalist circles. It is commonly believed that various elite groups in Persian society are organized in secret Freemason lodges under the control of the British, who use them to advance their secret designs to control world affairs. Groups accused of being controlled by the Freemasons include the courtiers, landowners, tribal chiefs, intellectuals, leading ulama, great merchants, contractors, influence-peddlers, political bosses, and most politicians, including Majles deputies and cabinet members.[94] Conspiracy theorists point to the role of well-known Masons like Sayyed Jamal al-Din Afghani, Mirza Malkam Khan Nazem al-Dawla, Sayyed Hasan Taqizada as evidence that the Persian Constitutional Revolution, like the French Revolution, was designed and perpetrated by the Freemasons and Illuminate. Freemasons are thought to have played also an important part in the founding of the Pahlavi dynasty.[95]

The main conspiracy theory relating to the Baha'i Faith is based on a forged document attributed to Prince Dimitri Dolgorukov ("Kinyaz Dalgoroki"), the Russian minister in Persia in 1846–54. The document, purporting to be a memoir in which the Prince describes how he created the Babi/Baha'i religion as a way of weakening Shi'ism and Persia, first circulated in Tehran in various forms in the late 1930s. Since then it has been widely cited in Muslim anti-Baha'i polemics as evidence that the Baha'i Faith was controlled first by the Russians and later by the British and\or Americans. A number of editions of this work have been printed, sometimes modified to reflect political developments.[96] However, a number of scholars have refuted the authenticity of this document, including 'Abbas Eqbal, Ahmad Kasrawi, Mahmud Mahmud, Mojtaba Minovi, and Abd-Allah Mostawfi.[97] In the 1970s the relative prosperity of the Persian Baha'is and the rumor that they numbered about three million (ten times the real figure) led to the belief that the Baha'is had conspired to buy Persia. Proof was adduced from the very extensive holdings of several Baha'i businessmen, one of whom managed to buy a large share of Saderat Bank, which had hundreds of branches throughout the country. Furthermore, the fact that the Baha'i world headquarters is located in Haifa, Israel, linked the Baha'i Faith to a supposed world Zionist conspiracy. Thus, for the conspiracy theorists, the Baha'i Faith is a Zionist political organization, not a religion. Some authors also see connection between the Baha'i Faith and both Freemasonry and Islamic fundamentalism. Thus, for example, the same Baha'i businessman is also accused of funding the Islamic Revolution.[98]

Those who believe in the international Jewish conspiracy to dominate the world find their proof in the *Protocols of the Elders of Zion*, a document forged by the Tsarist secret police but still widely accepted as authentic in the Middle East.[99] The Zionist conspiracy is thought to have supported the "despotic" rule of the shah. Thus, for example, it was believed that the soldiers who massacred "thousands" of innocent people on Black Friday (8 September 1978) were Israelis.[100] Other conspiracy theorists argue that Israel supported the Islamic Revolution in order to weaken her only potential rival in the region by replacing the shah's regime with the "vulnerable and dependent Islamic regime."[101]

The supposed Zionist and Baha'i conspiracy is often assumed to be connected to Freemasonry as well.[102] Thus, in 1979, a stenciled sign appeared on Tehran's street walls announcing the formation of an organization to fight against the conspiracy of Zionism, Baha'ism, and Freemasonry (Sazman-e zedd-e Sahyunist, zedd-e Baha'iyat, wa zedd-e Feramasoneri-ye Iran).

Unmasking Conspiracy Theories

Since the beginning of the 20th century, Persians from all walks of life and of all ideological orientations have relied on conspiracy theories as a basic mode for understanding politics and history. The covert intervention of the great powers in Iran's affairs in modern times has led Persians to interpret their history in terms of yet more elaborate and more devious conspiracies. The acceptance of such theories by ordinary people, the political elite, and even the rulers themselves who felt incapable of preventing or halting the rumored activities of foreign conspirators has, in turn, influenced the course of modern Persian history.

Although blaming others for one's own failure often serves an important social-psychological function, the conspiratorial mind-set has

proved, at times, to be highly dysfunctional; it has turned into a political
malaise in modern Persia, rendering the body politic incapable of
responding rationally and effectively to internal and external challenges
at times of crisis. An illusory sense of loss of control and learned help-
lessness creates "multiple psychological deficits" and leads people to
abandon any efforts to face social and political problems.

Although the Pahlavi Shahs as well as the leaders of the nationalist
and Islamic movements, Dr. Muhammad Mosaddeq and Ayatollah
Ruhollah Khomeini, as well as a large number of political figures and
members of the middle class have been highly receptive to conspiracy
theories, an increasing number of intellectuals have realized the negative
impacts of a conspiratorial mind-set. Realizing the dysfunctional effects
of conspiracy theories and, more specifically, that such theories become
self-fulfilling prophecies, a number of politicians and intellectuals have
attempted in the latter part of the 20th century to unmask and discredit the
proliferating repertoire of Persian blame placing schemata.[103] Notable
among them was Amir Asad Allah Alam, a close confidant and the court
minister of the late Shah, who not only revealed, in his invaluable diaries,
the Shah's belief in a wide range of conspiracy theories, but also underlined its damaging effects at the time of crisis.

Ironically, the effect of the belief in conspiracy theory in the making
of the 1977–79 revolution has been largely neglected. The first stage of
the revolution began when, following the victory of Jimmy Carter in the
presidential election of 1976, the Shah declared "It seems our days are
numbered." Meanwhile, Khomeini stated "The root of the malicious tree
of the Pahlavi dynasty is out of the soil—get united and throw it away."[104]
Furthermore, in his open message, he repeatedly referred to the "opportunity" that Carter's human rights policy has created for political mobilization against the Shah's regime. It was at this critical historical moment
that Alam called the Shah's attention to his earlier experience with the
Kennedy administration, when he was the prime minister and Khomeini
led widespread urban riots against the Shah. In this crisis the Shah was
hesitant to give the "shoot to kill order" because of his belief that the
movement was a British or a Freemason scheme. According to Alam:

> For some time we discussed the extent of foreign interference
> in our affairs, and how the American—Kennedy that is—

helped Amini to achieve power. I remarked that any manner of foreign backed conspiracy could always be thwarted if a few determined people were in the right places . . . . I ran through the events of 1963, how violent disorders broke out on 5 June following Khomeini's arrest; how HIM had rung me to ask what action I intended to take . . . how I told Your Majesty that I would hit them where it hurt . . . . There was no alternative. Had we backed down, the rioting would have spread to every corner of Iran and our regime would have collapsed in abject surrender. [emphasis added][105]

On the opposition camp, Mahdi Bazargan, the leader of the Iran Liberation Movement and the first prime minister after the 1979 Revolution, criticized the conspiratorial mind-set among Persians. Debunking the conspiracy theorists who attributed the Revolution to the American and British machination, Bazargan has openly declared that like other great movements in history, the leaders of the Iranian Revolution used Carter's pressure for human rights to mobilize the people and lead them to seize power.[106]

Excessive national preoccupation with conspiracy theories has contributed to the wide popularity of Iraj Pezeshkzad's comic classic of modern Persian fiction, *My Uncle Napoleon,* and a television serial based on it that was aired in the 1970s. Pezeshkzad's satire of this deeply paranoid patriot "has led to a Persian equivalent of the term 'Dear Uncle Napoleon–itis' being adopted as a name for such readiness to see conspiracy theories and the hidden hand of the West behind any and every local Iranian event."[107] Uncle Napoleon, a veteran officer of Gendarmerie in the South of Persia who lives in his daydream of an imaginary clash between his regiment and a British contingent in the South, believes that the British agents, including Indian pawns (who were at the time under British rule), would follow him to his grave to retaliate for his anti-British expeditions of the 1910s. "Staring into space with the same seraphic smile on his face," Dear Uncle relates a captivating memory with which he had lived for 30 years:

Yes, I've done my human and patriotic duty, and I was aware of the consequences. You think I didn't know what it means to fight with the English? You think I didn't know they'd block my career? You think I didn't know they'd never forget their hatred and enmity for me! On the contrary, I knew all this but I anointed my body with the fat of every hardship and humility and I fought . . . how many go-betweens they've set up, how many people they've sent, well, never mind . . . I remember my last commission in Mashhad . . . . One day toward sunset I was walking home . . . . Yes, just as I was going along I saw someone like an Indian trailing me. Well I paid no attention: then in the evening I was at home and there was a knock at the door. A private went to the door . . . He went to the door and came back and said 'There's an Indian come who says he's on the pilgrimage, but a problem's turned up and he wants to talk to the master for a moment.' I imme-diately suspected he was one of their pawns . . . . I swear by the soul of Layli I didn't even go to the door . . . I shouted 'Tell the gentleman he can only see my corpse' . . . I wasn't even prepared to say one word to him."[108]

However, as the author himself has experienced on various occa-sions, many readers of the satire "have taken the novel not so much as a lampooning of such paranoia but as a confirmation of the lasting rele-vance of such attitudes as a way of interpreting Iranian political life."[109]

As Pezeshkzad's personal experience clearly shows, unmasking and refuting theories that seem coherent and that are maintained tenaciously for emotional reasons is extremely difficult. Traditional scientific asser-tions are verifiable or falsifiable by external substantiation. But the appeal of conspiracy theories lies in their subjective emotional truth to believers, rather than in objective historical truth. Thus unmasking of the conspira-torial mind-set with its "inherent surreptitiousness and treachery, unsur-prisingly also involves internal, rather than the external criteria of truth: the accounts have to carry the intimate conviction of the judges, not mere-ly correspond to the external facts."[110] Conspiracy theories may be con-sidered as systems of collective delusion and irrational insofar as their logic, their coherence, and their causal linkage are surrealistic. The logic of conspiracy theories, as Dieter Groh has pointed out, can only be refuted in the realm of the theory of action and history, and the motives exposed from a socio-psychological point of view. Thus they cannot be scientifically refuted, not at least as long as one maintains the scientific-historical assumptions of paradigms as developed and refined by Thomas Kuhn.[111] [emphasis added]

In the realm of the theory of action and history, conspiracy theories are constructed on the theme that the political life is a puppet show in which the strings of power are pulled and manipulated by the invisible hands of the puppeteer. It is believed that all major political events are, step by step and in all details, stage-managed by the hidden hands of the conspirators and that all politicians are their agents. In this drama of conspiracy, a significant role is played by the popular figures who pretend to oppose the interests of great powers. Thus, it is believed that all the great leaders who fight overtly and vigorously against imperialism and colonialism in Persia are merely pawns acting on the scene. What is simply wrong with this belief is the fact that it overlooks the unintended consequences of human action. People do make their histories themselves, but often not in the way they have intended.

Notes

1. See, for example, Daniel Pipes, *Hidden hand: Middle East Fear of Conspiracy* (New York, 1996),who calls Iran "The World's Most Conspiracy-Minded Country" (p. 76). See also Ervand Abrahamian, *Khomeinism: Essays on the Islamic Republic* (Berkeley, 1993).

2. For a more detailed discussion see below and an expanded version of the present article in Persian: "Tvahhom-i Tawte'a," in *Goftegou*, Summer 1995, pp. 7–45.

3. For excellent interdisciplinary treatment of conspiracy theories see C. Graumann and S. Moscovici, eds., *Changing Conceptions of Conspiracy* (New York, 1987), pp. 1–37, 51–90, 151–90, 245–51.

4. Abu'l-Qasem Ferdowsi, *Shahnama*, I, ed. J. Khaleghi-Motlagh (New York: Bibliotheca Persica, 1988), pp. 89–157.

5. H. Bahrani, *Madina al-Ma'ajez* (Tehran, 1874).

6. See, for example, Mehdiqoli Hedayat, *Gozaresh-e Iran*, 2nd ed. (Tehran, 1984), pp. 150–392.

7. Peter Avery, *Modern Iran* (London, 1965), p. 40.

8. Taqizada, as the Minister of Finance, was a member of the Iranian negotiating team and reluctantly signed the agreement. See Sayyed Hasan Taqizada, *Zendagi-e Tufani. Khaterat-e Sayyed Hasan-e Taqizada*, ed. Iraj Afsar (Tehran, 1989), pp. 225–26, 236–44; Jawad Shaikh al-Islami, "Qaziya-ye Tamdid-e Emtiyaz-e Naft-e Jonub," *Ayanda* 14/1 (1988), pp. 13–25.

9. For the genesis of these theories in France and Germany, see H. Schmidt, "Anti-Western and Anti-Jewish Tradition in German Historical Thought," in *Leo Beck Institute, Year Book* IV (1959), pp. 37–60.

10. See, for example, Mehdi Mojtahedi, *Iran wa Engelis* (Tehran, 1947), pp. 2–22; Sepehr, op. cit., pp. 6, 70–75.

11. For numerous examples, see Mo'assesa-ye Motale'at wa Pazhuheshha-ye Siasi, *Zohur wa Soqut-e Saltanat-e Pahlavi*, 2 vols. (Tehran, 1991), passim; for a satirical depiction of this attitude of paranoia about the British, see the novel and TV serial, Iraj Pezeshkzad, *My Uncle Napoleon [Da'ijan Napel'on]*, tr. by Dick Davis (Washington, D.C.: Mage Publishers, 1996). See also M. Tolu'i, *Tars az Engelis* (Tehran, 1991). For a long list of victims see Mohammad Torkaman, *Asrar-e qatl-e Razmara* (Tehran, 1991), pp. 17–20.

13. Jalil Bozorgmehr, ed., *Mosaddeq dar Mahkama-ye Nezami*, 2 vols. (Piedmont, Calif., 1986), II, pp. 682–83; Hosein Makki, *Tarikh-e Bist Sala-ye Iran*, 2nd ed., 5 vols. (Tehran, 1978–79), III, pp. 385–89; Mo'assesa-ye Motale'at wa Pazhuheshha-ye Siasi, op. cit., II, p. 255; Naser Maleki, *Asrar-e Soqut-e Iran, I, Akhundism* (n.p., n.d.), p. 168; Mohammad Reza Pahlavi, *Answer to History* (New York, 1980), p. 71; Anthony Parsons, *The Pride & the Fall: Iran, 1974–1979* (London, 1984), p. x; Isma'il Ra'in, *Hoquq begiran-e Engelis dar Iran* (Tehran,1967), pp. 420–48; Ja'far Shahri, *Tarikh-e ejtema'i-ye Tehran dar qarn-e sizdahom*, 6 vols. (Tehran, 1988–89), V, p. 309.

14. Ahmad Khan Malek Sasani, *Dast-e Penhan-e Siyasat-e Engelis dar Iran* (Tehran, 1952).

15. Ibid., pp. 1–6; see also Ra'in, 1967, op. cit., pp. 162–85; cf. Avery, op. cit., pp. 41–44.

16. Khan Malek Sasani, 1952, op. cit., pp. 19, 42–52, 104–05.

17. Ibid., pp. 7–12; Ra'in, 1967, op. cit., pp. 44–68; cf. Faridun Adamiyyat,

"Sarnevest-e Qa'em-Maqam," [The destiny of Qa'em Maqam], in idem, *Maqalat-e Tarikhi* (Tehran, 1973), pp. 5–27.

18. Khan Malek Sasani, 1952, op. cit., pp. 24–41; 'Ali Asghar Shamim, *Iran dar Dawra-ye Saltanat-e Qajar* (Tehran, 1964), pp. 125–26; cf. *Amir Kabir wa Iran* (Tehran, 1976), pp. 682–760.

19. Khan Malek Sasani, 1952, op. cit., pp. 63–68; cf. H. L. Rabino, *Masruta-ye Gilan az Yaddastha-ye Rabino be enzemam-e Waqaye-e Mashad dar 1330*, ed. M. Rowshan (Rasht, 1974), pp. 117–45.

20. Khan Malek Sasani, 1952, op. cit., pp. 102–04.

21. Ibid., pp. 100–102; Naser Maleki, op. cit., pp. 145–46; R. Pashutan, *Iran dar atas*, 2 vols. (Vienna, 1984), I, pp. 157–60, II, pp. 42–49; Ra'in, 1967, op. cit., pp. 97–112, 367–79; E. Safa'i, *Rahbaran-e mashrata*, I (Tehran, 1965), p. 16; Shamim, op. cit., pp. 109–10, 170.

22. Khan Malek Sasani, 1952, op. cit., pp. 78, 82–83; Ra'in, 1967, passim; Abu'l-Fazl Qasemi, *Oligarshi ya khanadanha-ye hokumatgar-e Iran*, four monographs on leading families of notables, including *Khanadan-e Firuz/Farmanfarma'ian* (Tehran, 1974), *Khanadan-e Amini* (Tehran, 1976), *Khanadan-e Emam Jom'a* (Tehran, 1978), and *Khanadan-e Hoveyda* (Tehran, 1979).

23. Mahmud Mahmud, *Tarikh-e Rawabet-e Siyasi-ye Iran wa Engelis dar Qarn-e Nuzdahom-e Miladi*, 8 vols. (Tehran, 1949–54), VI, pp. 332–38; Ra'in 1967, op. cit., pp. 97–112.

24. Mahmud, op. cit., VI, pp. 255, 370–71, 390–91; VII, pp. 181–83; VIII, pp. 37, 51–55, 181–206, 210–26.

25. Hosein Makki, *Mokhtasari az zendagani-e siasi-e soltan Ahmad Shah Qajar* (Tehran, 1944).

26. For an attempted coup d'état by Reza Khan in 1917, see Abu'l-Qasem Khan Kahhalzada, *Didaha wa Shanidaha*, ed. M. Kamran (Tehran: Nashr-e Farhang, 1984), pp. 299–308; for the actual involvement of the British, see Edmund Ironside, *High Road to Command: Diaries of Major-General Sir Edmund Ironside, 1920–22* (London, 1972), pp. 149, 160–61.

27. Ruh-Allah Khomeini, *Sahifa-ye Nur*, 18 vols. (Tehran, 1983), XIII, p. 151; cf. Mostawfi, op. cit., III, p. 325.

28. Bamdad, *Tarikh-e Rejal-e Iran*, I (Tehran, 1968), pp. 85–89; 'Abbasqoli Golsa'ian, "Yaddastha'i Chand Raje' be Marhum-e Dawar," in Syrus Ghani, ed., *Yadashtha-ye Doktor Qasem-e Ghani*, XI (London, 1984), pp. 607–52, pp. 637–46; Makki, 1978–79, op, cit., I, pp. 137–256; cf. Shaikh al-Islami, *Sima-ye Ahmad Shah Qajar*, I (Tehran, 1989), pp. 312–25, 444–45;

Ardeshir Reporter, "Khaterat," in Mo'assesa-ye Motale'at wa Pazhuheshha-ye Siasi, II, op. cit., pp. 146–59.

29. Jalal Al-e Ahmad, *Gharbzadagi* (Tehran, n.d.), p. 41; Golsha'iyan, op. cit., p. 647; Hosein Kay-Ostovan, *Siyasat-e Mowazana-ye Manfi* (Tehran, 1950), p. 34; Khomeini, op. cit., VI, pp. 182–87, XIII, pp. 151–52; Gholam Reza Mosawwer-Rahmani, *Kohna Sarbaz* (Tehran, 1985), pp. 440–47, 517–18; B. Nikbin, ed., *Gozasta Cheragh-e Rah-e Ayanda Ast* (Tehran, 1983), pp. 31–33; Mohammad Reza Pahlavi, 1961, p. 84; Shahri, op. cit., II, pp. 219–21, 629; cf. Mostawfi, op. cit., III, p. 325.

30. Dawlatababadi, op. cit., IV, pp. 289–91; Mohammad Taqi Haji-Busehri, "Ruh-Allah Musawi Khomeyni: Tofuliyat, sabawat, wa shabab," *Chasmandaz*, Fall 1988, pp. 12–37.

31. See Khomeini, I, op. cit., pp. 200, 268–69, XI, pp. 86–87, 125–26, XIII, pp. 151, 177; Hosein Razi, *Athar al-Hojja*, 2 vols. (Qom, 1953), I, pp. 24–36, 46–52, 114–116.

32. For the espionage tale see A. Zischka, *La guerre secrete pour le petrole* (Paris, 1934), pp. 20–32, 145–55; see also Abu'l-Fazl Lesani, *Tela-ye Siah ya Bala-ye Iran* (Tehran, 1950), pp. 578–79; cf. A. Hardinge, *A Diplomatist in the East* (London, 1928), pp. 278–79; R. Ferrier, *The History of the British Petroleum Company I, The Developing Years 1901–1932* (London, 1982), pp. 35–40; Mostafa Fateh, *Panjah Sal Naft-e Iran* (Tehran, 1956), pp. 250–59; Lesani, op. cit., pp. 42–86.

33. Hosein E'zam-Qodsi, *Ketab-e Khaterat-e Man,* 2 vols. (Tehran, 1963–70), II, pp. 669–71; Mehdiqoli Hedayat, *Khaterat wa khatarat* (Tehran, 1950), p. 462; Lesani, op. cit., pp. 378–82, 578; cf. Peter Avery, *Modern Iran* (New York, 1965), pp. 3–64; Mohammad Taqi Bahar, *Tarikh-e Mokhtasar-e Ahzab-e Siyasi*, 2 vols. (Tehran, 1944 and 1984), II, pp. 115–27, 187; Makki, 1978–79, op. cit., III, pp. 93–115; Mostawfi, III, op. cit., pp. 617–25.

34. Lesani, op. cit., pp. 135–214; Mohammad Mosaddeq, *Khaterat wa ta'allo-mat-e Mosaddeq*, ed. Iraj Afshar (Tehran, 1986), pp. 198–201; Nikbin, op. cit., pp. 38–40; Shahri, op. cit., II, p. 629; cf. Sayyed Hasan Taqizada, *Zendagi-e Tufani. Khaterat-e Sayyed Hasan-e Taqizada*, ed. Iraj Afsar (Tehran, 1989), pp. 225–26, 236–44; Jawad Shaikh al-Islami, "Qaziya-ye Tamdid-e Emtiyaz-e Naft-e Jonub," *Ayanda* 14/1 (1988), pp. 13–25.

35. Lesani, op. cit., pp. 353–93; Ja'far Mahdinia, *Zendagi-ye Siyasi-ye Razmara* (Tehran, 1984), pp. 167–71, 235–67; Shahri, op. cit., II, pp. 396–404.

36. Anwar Khama'i, *Khaterat-e Doktor Anwar-e Khama'i*, 3 vols. (Tehran, 1982–84), II, pp. 32–43, III, pp. 348–63; Khalil Maleki, *Khaterat-e Siyasi*, ed. Homa Katuzian (Hanover, 1981), pp. 466–67; Mohammad Mosaddeq,

Taqrirat-e Mosaddeq dar Zendan, ed. Iraj Afsar (Tehran, 1980), p. 133; R. Pashutan, *Iran dar Atash*, 2 vols. (Vienna, 1984), II, pp. 54–55; Ehsan Tabari, *Kazhraha* (Tehran, 1987), pp. 46–49.

37. Torkaman, op. cit., pp. 443–45.

38. Pashutan, op. cit., II, pp. 40–41, 54–55.

39. Siyavosh Bashiri, *Tufan dar 57*, I (n.p., n.d.), pp. 22–26, 92–93, 422–23; N. Maleki, op. cit., pp. 79–86, 257–60, 357–92; R. Dreyfuss and T. LeMarc, "Muslim Brotherhood: London's Shocktroops for the New Dark Ages," *Executive Intelligence Review*, 8–14 May 1979, pp. 14–31; for a refutation of this allegation, see Sayyed Hadi Khosrowsahi *Negahi be Asnad-e Serri-e Engelis* (Rome, 1984).

40. Taqizada, op. cit., pp. 362–64.

41. 'Asad Allah 'Alam, *The Shah and I*, ed. and tr. by Alinaqi Alikhani (London, 1991), p. 239.

42. Ibid., p. 122.

43. Ibid., p. 176.

44. Mohammad Reza Pahlavi, 1980, op. cit., p. 71.

45. Idem, *Mission for my Country* (London, 1961), pp. 82–110, 126; see also Pashutan, op. cit., II, pp. 140–64, who believes that even the oil nationalization movement was a British design; for similar accusations against Mosaddeq from the Tudeh Party, see Khama'i, op. cit., III, pp. 206–13, 273–82; Tabari, op. cit., pp. 32, 352; cf. Mosaddeq, 1986, op. cit., pp. 338–97.

46. Pahlavi, 1980, p. 15.

47. Ashraf Pahlavi, *Faces in the Mirror* (Englewood Cliffs, N.J., 1980), pp. 199–200.

48. 'Abd al-Rahman, *The Betrayal of Iran* (n.p., 1979), p. 51; Jalal Ahanchian, *Tarh-e Soqut-e yak Padshah* (Mill Valley, Calif., 1982), pp. 19–21.

49. Bashiri, op. cit., pp. 53–95; Pashutan, op. cit., II, pp. 311–21; Shoja' al-Din Shafa, 1985, op. cit., II, pp. 1119–21, III, pp. 1669–78.

50. Parsons, op. cit., p. x.

51. Hosein Malek, *Nabard-e Perozhaha-ye Siyasi dar Sahna-ye Iran* (Tehran, 1981), app. pp. 7–10.

52. Pashutan, op. cit., II, pp. 322–27.

53. Robert Dreyfuss, *Hostage to Khomeini* (New York, 1980), pp. viii–x; Idem and LeMarc, op. cit., pp. 14–31; Lyndon LaRouche, *The Final Defeat of*

Ayatollah Khomeini (New York, 1982), pp. II–III; for the influence of these theories on Persian authors, see Bashiri, I, pp. 53–95, 410–11; Shafa, 1985, op. cit., III, pp. 1740, 1858–59.

54. Graumann and Moscovici, op. cit., pp. 28–30; Muriel Atkin, "Myths of Soviet-Persian Relations," in N. Keddie and M. Gasiorowski, eds., *Neither East nor West* (New Haven, 1990), pp. 100–14.

55. Makki, 1978–79, op. cit., III, p. 9; Mostawfi, op. cit., II, p. 357–59.

56. Pseudo– Abu'l-Qasem Lahuti Kermansahi, *Sarh-e Zendagani-e Man* (Tehran, 1953); Donald Wilber, *Adventures in the Middle East* (Princeton, 1986), p. 191; E'zam-Qodsi, op. cit., II, pp. 392–408.

57. Pahlavi, 1961, op. cit., p. 31.

58. Malek, 1981, op. cit., pp. 14, 51.

59. Daneshjuyan-e Peyrow-e Khatt-e Emam, *Asnad-e Lana-ye Jasusi*, 70 vols. (Tehran, 1980–86), XXVII, pp. 2, 66, 70–71, 136–41, 154.

60. 'Abd al-Hosein Meftah, *Rasti Birang Ast* (Paris, 1984), pp. 25, 41, 43; Pashutan, op. cit., II, pp. 322–23.

61. Daneshjuyan-e Peyrow-e Khatt-e Emam, op. cit., XXVII, p. 130.

62. Malek, op. cit., 1981, appendix, p. 10.

63. Pahlavi, 1980, op. cit., p. 145.

64. Mark Gasiorowski, "The 1953 Coup d'État in Iran," *IJMES* 19/3 (1987), pp. 261–86; Kermit Roosevelt, *Countercoup. The Struggle for the Control of Iran* (New York, 1979), passim; Wilber, op. cit., pp. 187–95; C. Woodhouse, *Something Ventured* (London, 1982), pp. 104–35.

65. Martin Herz, "Some Intangible Factors in Iranian Politics," American Embassy, Tehran, to Department of State, no. A-702 (June 15, 1964), p. 9.

66. Ahmad Ashraf, "State and Agrarian Relations before and after the Iranian Revolution, 1960–1990," in F. Kazemi and J. Waterbury, eds., *Peasants and Politics in the Modern Middle East* (Miami, 1991), pp. 278–84.

67. Malek, 1981, op. cit., appendix, p. 7.

68. Khomeini, op. cit., IV, pp. 24; V, pp. 23, 136; and VI, p. 181; see also H. Tavanayan-e Fard, *Tawte'aha-ye eqtesadi-ye amperialism dar Iran* (Tehran, 1985), pp. 444–93, pp. 131–33, 360–64; Mo'assesa-ye Pazhuheshha-ye Siyasi, op. cit., II, p. 226.

69. 'Ali Davani, *Nahzat-e Ruhaniyun-e Iran*, 8 vols. (Tehran, 1980), VI, pp. 331–70; *Keyhan-e Farhangi* 5/6 (1989), p. 32–35; M. Raf'at, *Takhti Mard-e Hamisha Javid* (Tehran, 1987), pp. 109–45; A. Sa'idiyan, *Zendagi-nama-ye*

101 tan az Qahramanan-e Enqelab-e Khalq-e Iran (Tehran, 1979), pp. 64, 132.

70. Pahlavi, 1980, op. cit., pp. 171, 173.

71. Ibid., p. 155.

72. Nur al-Din Kianuri, "The arduous path of the Persian revolution," *World Marxist Review* 26/3 (March 1983), pp. 30–36; "Siyasatha-ye now este'mari," *Danesju* 24/1 (1976), pp. 34–57.

73. F. Dana, *Amperializm wa Forupashi-ye Keshavarzi dar Iran* (Tehran, 1979), pp. 46–121; Baqer Mo'meni, *Eslahat-e Arzi wa Jang-e Tabaqati dar Iran* (Tehran, 1980), pp. 504–11.

74. *Iran Times*, March 15, 1991, p. 10.

75. M. Arasi, "Te'ori-ye tawte'a wa Tawte'azadagi," *Sahand*, no. 7 (1986), p. 4.

76. Babak, "Te'ori-ye Tawte'a ya Tawte'a dar 'Amal," *Kavosh, no.* 2 (nd.), pp. 32–35. Enqelabi-ye Baynalmelali, *Bayaniya* (n.p.), 1 May 1984; "Qachaq-e aslaha wa Faribkari-e Amperialstha," *Payam-e Feda'i*, May 1986, pp. 22–24, 46; Homa Nateq, "Yaran-e Mottahed dar Kudeta wa Enqelab," *Zaman-e now*, no. 8 (1985), pp. 11–22.

77. Khomeini, op. cit., XI, pp. 12–17; XII, pp. 133–41, 270–73; Daneshjuyan-e Peyrow-e Khatt-e Emam, op. cit., various issues, including XII, pp. 1–11; XVII, pp. 1–6; XVIII, pp. 1–4.

78. Abu'l-Hasan Banisadr, *My Turn to Speak: Iran, the Revolution, and Secret Deals with the U.S.* (Washington, D.C., 1991).

79. Ahmad Fardid, "Sadeq-e Hedayat dar Chala Harz-e Adabiyat-e Faransa," *Ettela'at*, 21 February 1973, p. 19.

80. Reza Davari, *Enqelab-e Eslami wa Waz'-e Konuni-e 'Alam* (Tehran, 1962); Idem, *Shemmaļi az Tarikh-e Gharbzadagi-e Ma* (Tehran, 1984).

81. Zabih Behruz, "Dibacha," introduction to Aslan Ghaffari, *Qessa-ye Sekandar wa Dara* (Tehran, 1964), pp. II–LXXIV; Ahmad Hami, *Safar-e Jangi-e Eskandar-e Maqduni be Iran wa Hendustan, Bozorgtarin Dorugh-e Tarik Ast* (Tehran, 1975).

82. Zabih Behruz, 1964, op. cit., pp. XXVIII–XXIX; Idem, *Taqwim wa Tarikh dar Iran* (Tehran, 1952), pp. 10–13.

83. Hosein Malek, *Tawallod-e Ghulha*, 3rd ed. (Paris, nd.), pp. 57–65.

84. Ibid., pp. 9–10, 29–53.

85. Ibid., pp. 68–71.

86. Khomeini, op. cit., I, pp. 86–92, 172; Jalal Al-e Ahmad, *Gharbzadagi*

(Tehran, n.d.), pp. 22–42; Z. Qorbani, *Elal-e Adam-e Pishraft-e Eslam wa Enhetat-e Moslemin* (Tehran, 1982), pp. 421–70.

87. 'Ali Shari'ati, *Bazshenasi-e Hawiyat-e Irani-ye Eslami* (Tehran, 1982), pp. 236–38; see also Pasutan, op. cit., I, pp. 121–25.

88. Pahlavi, 1980, op. cit., p. 145.

89. Shoja' al-Din Shafa, 1983, *Tawzih al-Masael, Pasokha'i be Porseshha-ye Hezar-sala* (Paris, 1983), p. 58.

90. Ibid., pp. 61–62.

91. Ibid., pp. 86–89.

92. Ibid., pp. 47–48, 89–90.

93. Ibid., pp. 89–90, 920–22; Bashiri, op. cit., I, pp. 408–11; N. Maleki, op. cit., pp. 1–8.

94. Esma'il Ra'in, 1969, op. cit., III, pp. 580–636.

95. Bashiri, op. cit., I, pp. 48–52; Mahmud, op. cit., V, pp. 25–34, VII, pp. 2–42; Ra'in, *Anjomanha-ye Serri dar Enqelab-e Mashrutiyat* (Tehran, 1976), pp. 41–140; and Ebrahim Safa'i, *Rahbaran-e Mashruta*, 2 vols. (Tehran, 1965–67), I, pp. 4, 15, 41–63, 122–31, II, pp. 227–45; Idem, *Asnad-e Mashruta* (Tehran, 1973), pp. 95–112.

96. See Mortaza; E'zam-Qodsi, op. cit., II, pp. 549–80; Mostawfi, op. cit., I, pp. 42–44; for a recent appearance of the document in a monarchist newspaper, see *Shahfaraz-e Aryan*, no. 32 (February 1989), pp. 2–7.

97. 'Abbas Eqbal, *Majalla-ye Yadgar* 5/8–9 (1949), p. 148; Ahmad Kasrawi, *Baha'igari* (Tehran, 1944), pp. 88–90; Mahmud Mahmud, op. cit., VIII, p. 143; Mojtaba Minovi, "Sharh-e Zendagi-ye Man," *Rahnama-ye Ketab* 6/1–2 (1963), pp. 22–26; Abd-Allah Mostawfi, op. cit., I, pp. 42–44.

98. Bashri, op. cit., I, pp. 9–26, 45–52.

99. Norman Cohen, *Warrant for Genocide. The Myth of the Jewish World Conspiracy and the Protocols of the Elders of Zion* (Chicago, 1981).

100. 'Ali Davani, *Nahzat-e ruhaniyun-e Iran*, 8 vols. (Tehran, 1980), VIII, pp. 49–59; another theory identifies them as Palestinians; Shafa, *Jenayat wa Mokafat*, 4 vols. (Paris, 1985), III, pp. 1789–91.

101. Shafa, op. cit., III, pp. 1697–744.

102. M. Zavosh, *Rabeta-ye Feramasoneri ba Sahyunism wa Amperialism* (Tehran, 1982).

103. See, for example M. Arasi, "Te'ori-ye Tawte'a wa Tawte'azadagi," *Sahand*, no. 7 (1986), pp. 1–19; Mahmud 'Enayat, "Az Dast-e Namar'i-ye Engelis,"

Ruzegar-e Now 9/8 (October 1990), pp. 79–85; Idem, "Zir-e Kasa Nim Kasaist," in Payam-e Ashna 3/22 (November 1991), pp. 21–24; Martin Herz, op. cit., pp. 8–9; Mehdi Mojtahedi, *Iran wa Engelis* (Tehran, 1947), pp. 2–40, 72–75; Muhammad Mohit Tabataba'i, "Dar Mian-e Haqq wa Batel," and "Az Mazmum ta Mahmud," reprinted in Ra'in, 1967, op. cit., pp. 449–54 and 458–61; Mostawfi, op. cit., III, pp. 571–75, 642–49.

104. For the Shah's statement, see A. Ashraf and A. Banuazizi, op. cit., p. 4. For Khomeini's statement, see A. Badamchian, "Tarikh-e engelab az zaban-e farzandan-e engelab," in *Rezalat*, 25 January 1966, p. 7.

105. Asad Allah 'Alam, *The Shah and I*, ed. and tr. by Alinaqi Alikhani (London, 1991), p. 280.

106. Mahdi Bazargan, *Inqelab-e Iran dar Dwo Harakat*, 3rd ed. (Tehran, 1984), pp. 12, 58–59.

107. Iraj Pezeshkzad, *My Uncle Napoleon*, op. cit., p. 12.

108. Ibid., pp. 193–94.

109. Ibid., p. 12.

110. Henry Zukier, "The Conspiratorial Imperative," in C. Graumann and S. Moscovici, eds., *Changing Conceptions of Conspiracy*, op. cit., p. 92.

111. Dieter Groh, "The Temptation of Conspiracy Theory...." in C. Graumann and S. Moscovici, eds., *Changing Conceptions of Conspiracy*, op. cit., p. 4.

Challenges to Turkish Democracy in the Decade of the Nineties*

HEATH LOWRY

*"An imbalance between rich and poor is the oldest
and most fatal ailment of republics."*
Plutarch

While in recent years a great deal of attention has been focused on Turkey's economic transformation from a statist to a free-market economy, as well as on its potential role as a democratic and economic model for new states that have emerged in the wake of the collapse of the eastern bloc, relatively little if any serious examination has been directed at the impact of these changes on Turkey itself. The present paper is a preliminary attempt at opening such a discourse.

The hypothesis around which it is developed is a relatively simple, albeit somewhat controversial, one. Namely, that until recently the development of democratic institutions in the Turkish Republic has been hampered by the existence of a series of elite-imposed ideological taboos (designed to buttress the state ideology) on a variety of subjects including history, religion, ethnicity, pan-Turkism, press freedom, and the Atatürk legacy, or *Atatürkçülük*. Further, in the past two decades an ever-widen-

---

*Although this paper was originally delivered as a lecture at Princeton University in May of 1993, it does forecast many developments of the past year, e.g., changes affected by the coming to power of the avowedly Islamicist REFAH Party.

ing discussion of these long-forbidden subjects has begun, with the result being that each is now fully represented on the nation's agenda. Ironically, with the removal of taboos, Turkish democracy can be said to have fully come of age, while, at the same time and somewhat paradoxically, the growth into a more mature democracy now presents a series of challenges to the very fabric of Turkish society. Stated differently, with the removal of the taboos the central elite's ideological foundations are threatened. Voices long muted now seek to draw Turkey into a variety of directions: groups openly espouse the return to the Şer'iyat (Islamic law), others call for the creation of a Kurdish state on Turkish soil, yet others voice the long-suppressed dream of a Turkish state stretching from China to Europe—all sound their appeal to the populace.

Were these developments transpiring in a political vacuum it might well be possible that time and cool judgment would ultimately succeed in shaping a new rationale and policy formulations for the state. But this is not the case. To the contrary, they are paralleled by even more extensive changes in neighboring countries that exacerbate developments in Turkey.

While observers of Turkey have long known that the country's neighborhood was less than desirable, the added chaos resulting from the collapse of the Soviet Union and the Eastern Bloc, together with Iranian efforts to export their brand of Islamic fundamentalism to secular Turkey, the still-unsettled aftermath of the Gulf War and the revitalized Kurdish Question it spawned, not to mention the rekindling of ethnic-religious hatred in the Balkans, all point to the fact that a once-borderline neighborhood is rapidly degenerating. In the midst of this, Turkey stands with one foot in Europe and the other on less than firm ground. It also stands as the one former empire in the region that has successfully (although not painlessly) made the transition from an oligarchy to a democracy and from a highly centralized to a free-market economy. As such it could well serve as a model for both newly-freed former Soviet states and the troubled Balkans. However, before any of this may occur, Turkey must first ensure that its own house is in order.

While in no way intended to downplay the importance of the massive structural changes in the Turkish economy that have been achieved in the past decade, the present paper is designed as a cautious preliminary step to identify some of the more controversial ideological currents now abroad in Turkey, to pinpoint their causes, and to trace their developments during the past two decades. It is offered in the hope that viewed from a distance, through foreign, albeit sympathetic, eyes, the outline of a larger picture may begin to emerge. It is relatively easy for those living in North America and following Turkey via the western and Turkish press to keep somewhat abreast of the larger picture. It is less easy to accurately describe its component elements without experiencing life in Turkey on a daily basis. Consequently, the reader's indulgence is sought in advance for any shortcomings from which the present analysis may suffer.

The Historical Taboo

In keeping with my own occupational prejudices, I open this discussion with some comments on what might be termed the taboo concerning the official historical thesis (*resmi tarih tezi*) of the Turkish Republic in its first half-century of existence and then turn to an examination of the challenges it faces in today's rapidly changing world.

A careful perusal of the high-school history texts that were used in Turkey in the first two generations of the Republic points to the inescapable conclusion that successive generations of students were exposed to a highly ethnocentric view of the world focused almost exclusively on the Turks and their history. Little or no attention was paid to the rest of the world and almost none at all to the histories of Turkey's neighbors, except insofar as they had once been part of the Ottoman Empire.

With Ottoman history itself, a great deal of attention was paid to the so-called Golden Age of the fifteenth and sixteenth centuries, and relatively little to the stagnant centuries of decline that followed it. Literally no attention at all was directed to the underlying causes of the Balkan and Arab nationalisms, and the history of these movements was treated solely as the result of rapacious European powers seeking to dismember the Sick Man of Europe. Consequently, the breakup of the Pax Ottomanica was the result of betrayal of various subject peoples, who were assumed to have lived an almost blissful existence under centuries of benevolent

Ottoman rule.

Needless to say, this view of the past was not shared by the often vehemently nationalist historiographies that developed among the former Ottoman subjects. There, the expounders followed the exact opposite approach and, neglecting entirely the period of Ottoman greatness, focused exclusively upon the status quo under which their own break-away movements had grown.

What resulted was a classic lack of mutual understanding, mitigated to some extent by the fact that Turkey's eyes in the first five decades of the Republic's existence were focused inward. That is, it paid relatively little attention to the neighborhood surrounding it and concentrated instead on the attempted transfer of a once-backward Ottoman province into the nation-state of Turkey.

History and its teaching were first viewed by the guardians of *Atatürkçülük* as a tool to be employed by the state in shaping the minds of the young to be good Turkish citizens. Year after year Turkish students memorized the same facts and dates and successfully passed their history courses. Indeed, the most obvious result of such education was to foster in its recipients a deep and abiding dislike for the study of history.

This official state history continued almost unchallenged until the early 1970s, when successive coalition partners began to control the Ministry of Education, and thereby the education curriculums, thus advancing their own varied belief systems on the nation's youth. I vividly recall standing before a class of close to three hundred Boğaziçi University students in 1975 and attempting to answer a student's query as to whether the history he had been taught as a junior in high school or that he had learned as a senior was correct. His well-chosen example concerned passages in the two textbooks he had used during those two years. One, in discussing the Central Asia ruler Timurlenk (Tamerlane), described him as "a great Turkish leader and a Muslim," whereas the second referred to him as "an unbeliever and an enemy of the Turks." Clearly, cracks were beginning to appear in the *resmi tarih tezi* of the state.

This ostrich-like approach to the past might well have continued to serve the nation's needs were it not for a whole series of outside factors whose impact began to be felt in Turkey in the seventies and eighties.

One such event was the advent of Armenian terrorist attacks directed principally against Turkish diplomats in the name of an historical grievance which few Turks even knew existed. Turco-Armenian relations was simply not a subject that had ever warranted coverage in the country's textbooks. More currently, the revival of the Macedonian Question and the Bosnian-Serbian conflict has sent policy makers in Ankara scrambling in a search for information about an aspect of the Ottoman past which likewise was known only to the specialist.

Clearly, as Turkey begins to shift from its long-held foreign policy of maintaining the status quo toward one that projects it into a role as a regional power and leader, the taboo associated with an open and free discussion of its historical past (warts and all) is going to have to disappear. The question is what role, if any, are Turkish historians, trained as narrow specialists on specific periods of Ottoman history, going to be able to contribute to what must ultimately emerge as a more rational study of the past. The failure of Turkish academia to address the histories of neighboring peoples in a meaningful way is exemplified by the fact that, as late as 1993, there was not a single course offered in modern Greek history, or for that matter in the contemporary Greek language, at any Turkish university. This situation existed despite a plethora of unresolved bilateral problems that have marred relations between Turkey and its Aegean neighbor. By way of contrast, there are major programs in Turkish Studies at the University of Crete and at the University of Nicosia in Cyprus. The challenge is for Turkey to begin training scholars as specialists in other fields of history, rather than focusing its interests exclusively on surviving Ottoman sources.

The Religious Taboo

The laicism espoused as official ideology in the opening years of the Republic traditionally bore a far closer relationship to the atheism of the former Soviet Union than it did to the western concept of secularism. Islam in Turkey, like all religious expression in the Soviet Union, was treated as a dangerous current which, although impossible to eradicate, had to be placed firmly under the control of the state. Widespread destruction of places of worship, together with total government control of all religious functionaries, was inherent in both systems. Overt religiosity was tolerated but discouraged under both systems and successive generations of elite Turks and Soviets grew to adulthood associating flagrant religious practice with backwardness and disloyalty to the state.

The first cracks in Turkey's religious taboo appeared in the 1950s, when politicians began to realize that proper playing of the religious card was an effective way of garnering votes. Thus, throughout the 1950s, the Menderes governments granted ever-increasing concessions to the country's religious conservative element, a fact that in no small part accounted for the width of the victories they enjoyed in successive elections. Following the military interventions of 1960 and 1971, later generations of politicians (Demirel and Ecevit among them in the 1960s and 1970s) continued to play for the religious vote. Yet, every Turk knew that the ultimate protectors of *Atatürkçülük*, the Turkish military, frowned on such expressions, and, indeed, each succeeding military intervention and its aftermath proved the point.

These developments transpired simultaneously with major influxes of peasants to the urban centers of Istanbul, Ankara, and Izmir. These newcomers, largely untouched by the elite's secularism, brought their own more conservative religious practices with them. This had a dual effect. On the one hand, it challenged the underlying principles of Turkey's westernization process, which was based on the theory that a westernized, modern urban elite's values would "trickle down" to the rural population. On the other hand, urban population movements meant that the religious values of the first and second generation peasants began to figure prominently in what had previously been the preserves of the secularized urban elite. For example, the population of Istanbul grew twelvefold in the generation between 1960 and 1990, from under one million to over twelve million. While the urban elite may have continued to shun overt religious practices such as attendance at the Friday noon prayers, the new arrivals did not. What had begun as an attempt to spread the values of Istanbul to the Anatolian population was transformed into the "Anatolization" of Istanbul.

Ironically, it was the most secular of the guardians of *devlet* (state), the Turkish military, that ultimately was to open the floodgates of religious expression and destroy the remaining taboos associated with it. Following the September 12, 1980 military intervention, the de facto head of state, General Kenan Evren, determined that a root cause of the terrorism that had plagued Turkey in the pre-intervention period was a lack of proper moral and ethical training on the part of the Turkish youth. Associating such training with religion, the solution of the military was not only to allow such training, but further to mandate religious education in the nation's public school system (Hughes, 1992: pp. 189–). At the very least this development signalled the end of the military's role as guardians of laicism and gave an impetus to the trends that had begun under conservative coalition governments of the 1970s. These were marked by a massive growth in everything from the building of mosques and *mescid*s (small mosques) to the blossoming of hundreds of additional *İmam-Hatip* schools in all corners of the country.

When combined with the fact that Turkey's Iranian neighbor had just undergone a massive fundamentalist revolution and with the appearance of a growing Saudi Arabian interest in "reconverting" Turkish Muslims to the true path of Islam, religious forces suddenly found themselves awash in funding. In the ensuing decade tens of thousands of poor students have had their educations financed by various Muslim groups, and the long-treasured pillar of secularism has been further weakened.

When one factors into the equation the role played by the late Turgut Özal, who between 1983 and 1993 served first as Prime Minister and then as President of Turkey, the extent to which the religious taboo has been broken becomes even more apparent. An openly practicing Muslim whose first foray into elected politics was an unsuccessful run for Parliament from Izmir in 1978, as a member of the religious National Salvation Party, Özal and an entire wing of the Motherland Party he formed in 1983 were closed tied to fundamentalist and *tarikat* (dervish fraternity) circles in Turkey. Thus in fifty years the leadership of Turkey has swung from the open agnosticism of Mustafa Kemal Atatürk to the openly Muslim stance of Turgut Özal. In the process, the long-held taboo vis-a-vis the overt practice of religion (typified by mosque attendance at the Friday noon prayers, fasting during the month of Ramazan, public *iftar yemekleri* [evening meals that break the Ramazan fasting] and making the pilgrimage to Mecca) has evaporated and in its place we see a

Turkey wherein religion looms ever larger on the agenda.

Shortly before his death in April of 1993, during speeches given during his last visit to Washington, D.C., President Özal repeatedly stressed his vision of a future in which the former Cold War East-West confrontation will be replaced by an ever widening circle of Muslim-Christian clashes. To his audiences there was no doubt that he was issuing these warnings as a Muslim leader of a country he viewed as part of the Muslim side of the equation. To say the least it is unthinkable that any of his predecessors who served as President of the Republic would ever have shared his stance in this regard, although many present-day Turkish politicians clearly express similar views in describing the failure of the west to intervene in Bosnia.

What has been the impact of the breaking of the religious taboo and what does it bode for the future of Turkey? Recent indications, including massive public demonstrations following the assassination of prominent columnist Uğur Mumcu (a devout secularist) point to a new possibility, that of a growing tension between those segments of the population still espousing Atatürk's secular vision and those identified with the growing Islamic revival in Turkey. The slogans voiced by the crowd of several hundred thousand mourners who carried Mumcu to his resting place were vociferously secular and went so far as to contrast the laicism of Mustafa Kemal Atatürk with the pro-Islamic leanings of Turgut Özal. All this occurred even before the official investigation of the Mumcu assassination began to point toward radical Turkish Muslim fundamentalists trained in Islamic Iran as the perpetrators of this and other assassinations of prominent secular intellectuals in the early 1990s.

While hopefully Özal's projected Islam-Christianity confrontation will not take the form of a Secularist-Islamic confrontation in Turkey, one fact is inescapable. There are signs of an ever-growing tension between the secularist segment of Turkish society (the elite and middle classes) on one side, and on the other, those identified as fundamentalists (a 1993 poll indicated that 63% of the population feel "Islamic values should have a higher place in society," and that 13% strongly agreed, and 15% somewhat agreed with the statement that "Turkey must be administered according to Şer'iyat laws." [PIAR, 1/29/1993: pp. 8–9]). It is for this latter group, i.e., the 28% of the population that currently either openly expresses, or leans towards, support for the imposition of the *Şer'iyat* laws in Turkey, that Islam as a way of life may offer a tempting alternative to a market economy in which they see little place for themselves.

While comparisons with Iran in the last days of the Shah's regime may well be unwarranted, there can be little doubt but that for most supporters of Khomeini it was less his religious appeal that garnered their support than a chance to alter a political system in which they had little voice or role. The gap that continues to grow between the relatively small group of Turks who are benefiting in a meaningful way from the country's new free-market economy, and the great multitude of the population who see only a decline in real buying power and savings due to a decade of runaway inflation, is a dangerous one (DEİK, 1991) and unless addressed promptly could pave the way for a state system in which Islam plays a far larger role.

The lifting of the religious taboo in Turkey coincided with the Iranian Revolution and for he generation of Turks who have come of age in the last decade (complete with several years of religious instruction in their educations), the possibility of an alternative form of government, in which the role of Islam is increased, may not be quite as alien as it is to their elders educated in the strict secularist tradition. The late Turgut Özal's oft-expressed view that religion is a personal matter may well have reflected his exposure to life in the United States. What it did not reflect was a clear understanding of Islam and the role that it traditionally plays in all aspects of the believers' lives.

Whatever the outcome, in 1990s religion is a factor in the political future of the Turkish Republic in a manner and to an extent that none of the founders of this state could have envisaged. A combination of factors, including politicians seeking votes, the naivety of the Turkish military when it came to social engineering, the example of Turgut Özal himself, and the increasing exercise of democratic values by the populace at large, have all combined to ensure that the role of religion in twenty-first century Turkey will be far different than that seen in the republic's first two generations. Whether or not Turks will follow the "Dark Voice" (Kara Ses) of the late Cemalettin Kaplan, a leader of the Turkish fundamentalists in Germany, or that of some yet unheard voice, religious expression in Turkey will never re-enter the Pandora's box from which it has been released. Paradoxically, this new-found freedom of religious expression is in fact yet another proof of the extent to which Turkish democracy has matured in the past four decades, while at the same time it holds the potential to alter the very system that gave it birth.

The Ethnicity Taboo

Central to the creation of Turkish nationalism, that is, to the ideological foundation of the state, was the well-entrenched taboo against any kind of emphasis on one's ethnicity. Such expression not only ran counter to the prevailing ideology that all Muslim citizens of Turkey were in fact ethnic Turks, it also carried the seeds of *bölücülük*, or separatism, the crime of promoting one group at the expense of another.

As the heartland of a once-mighty multiethnic empire, Anatolia at the end of World War I was a veritable melting pot of the many peoples who had lived under the Ottoman umbrella for centuries, including Turks, Kurds, Arabs, Greeks, Armenians, Jews, Circassians, Bosnians, and Albanians, to name just a few of the "seventy-two and a half *millets* in Turkey." Yet, just as the founders of the new state chose to reject Islam as a cohesive element in their nation-building process, so they chose to reject a geographic basis, that is, rather than uniting around the name "Anatolia" or Anatolians," they chose to name the state after the largest single group among the "seventy-two and a half *millets*" comprising the population. Overnight, a multitude of different peoples found that they were Turks. While the experience of the past seventy years has shown that in the case of most ethnic groups, the process of "Turkification" has been completed successfully and generally painlessly, this was clearly not so with the largest non-Turkish ethnic group: the Kurds. Successive revolts in 1925 and 1938, and the harsh reaction of a state fighting for its very survival, not to mention identity, created a situation in which any expression of Kurdishness was simply not tolerated.

Typified by extensive forced resettlement of Kurds in western Turkey, forced renaming of all Kurdish towns and villages in the 1940s, forced adoption of Turkish and Muslim as distinct from Kurdish proper names, legal prosecution of anyone engaging in any written expression of

Kurdish ethnicity (this was true for Turks as well as Kurds), the official state policy hardened into one which oft-times bordered on the comic if not the absurd. Countless books and articles, all of them falling into the realm of pseudo-scholarship, tried to show that there was no Kurdish language and therefore no Kurds. This process was complicated by the fact that as most Turks and Kurds shared the same religion (the majority of both are Sunni Muslims), intermarriage was possible and widespread. For those Kurds who found their way into the bureaucracy, the military or business, assimilation was relatively rapid and no one ever questioned or discriminated against them due to their Kurdish origin (Kahveci, 1987: p. 2). Nor, in reality, could there be such discrimination. For, if one officially does not recognize the existence of Kurds as a separate people, one does not have a great deal of room for ethnic discrimination. Stated differently, the cost of fully entering life in the new republic was the denial of one's ethnicity. To anyone willing to do so all doors were opened, and in the course of the past two generations up to half the ethnic Kurds have taken advantage of that open door and assumed their place as full members of Turkish society. This process failed, however, in those regions of southeastern Anatolia where ethnic Kurds not only were the overwhelming majority of the population, but which, because of their remoteness from the developing western regions of the country, had little impetus to Turkify. Far from Ankara and all too often used as a dumping ground for incompetent or corrupt administrators, the Kurdish residents seldom even bothered to learn Turkish. Neither the government nor the private sector took any interest to speak of in the southeast or in assimilating its Kurdish inhabitants. And while Turkification continued apace among those Kurds who left their homes and migrated west to the major urban centers in the hope of employment and a better life, those who remained behind were clearly left out of the "Turkish Dream."

This situation continued until the mid-eighties when then-Prime Minister Turgut Özal broke the ethnic taboo by openly acknowledging the existence of the Kurds as a separate ethnic group and even going so far as to identify himself as part Kurdish. Suddenly, the Pandora's box of ethnicity was open and the Kurdish Question was placed squarely on the Turkish agenda. When sometime thereafter (1991), then President Özal's spokesman, Ambassador Kaya Toperi announced in an interview on the

BBC that there at least 12 million Kurds among Turkey's fifty-seven million citizens, comprising over 20% of the population, the floodgates were fully opened. All of this came at a time when the collapse of the Soviet Union had placed ethnicity and the human and political rights of minorities high on everyone's agenda; and when, concurrent with a growing Kurdish separatist movement, the PKK, while based in neighboring Syria, Iraq, and Iran, clearly was gaining sympathy and support among Turkish Kurds as well.

Currently Turkey faces a "Kurdish issue" at least equal to that represented by the Sheikh Said Rebellion in 1925, or by the Dersim Revolt in 1938. There are important differences, however. In the 1990s, CNN instantly relays developments in southeastern Anatolia to a worldwide audience, whereas in 1925 or 1938 no one in the rest of the world paid significant attention to Turkey's harsh suppression of the Kurdish uprisings. Today, unlike in the past, several dozen human rights organizations not only monitor developments in Turkey, they use their voices to attempt to thwart Turkish participation in a variety of international forums until and unless the human rights of Turkey's Kurds are fully respected. In Europe particularly, Kurdish separatist groups are well organized and enjoy support among a variety of groups in Germany, Scandinavia, and France. In the 1990s, the world is far less likely to sit by and watch Turkey impose a military solution on this particular round of the Turkish-Kurdish imbroglio.

Nor does the problem necessarily end with the Kurds. Once the ethnicity taboo was lifted (a process simultaneously going on throughout the region), a variety of other voices began to make themselves heard in Turkey. Bosnian, Caucasian, and Azerbaijani Turkish voices are now being raised on behalf of their former kinspeople in the Balkans and the former Soviet Union. Simply put, ethnic politics have begun to make their presence felt in Turkey, and this adds an entirely new and potentially complicating element into Turkish foreign and domestic policy considerations.

The ultimate ethnic issue may well stem from the fact that the sentiments of those elements in the population identifying themselves as Turks (regardless of their roots) are beginning to feel threatened by the Kurdish Question and may well be prompted into action. Signs that this is happening are readily apparent in statements made by government leaders, including Özal's successor as President, Süleyman Demirel, who several times in recent years has warned against Turks buying weapons, Turks refusing to hire Kurds or firing those already employed, Turks refusing to patronize Kurdish-owned shops, refusing to rent to Kurds, etc. These actions are happening not in the southeast of the country but in the major urban centers of Istanbul, Ankara, Antalya, and Izmir.

Faced with the real possibility of increasing ethnic clashes in the not too distant future, Turkey's elected leaders seem too paralyzed to take any decisive action. While the Demirel-İnönü coalition government began well—both the coalition protocol and the governmental program called for significant liberalization of policies affecting Kurds—they soon found themselves caught in a dilemma. Given the PKK-inspired cycle of violence, Turkish public opinion began to equate any response to demands for fuller Kurdish human rights with concessions to terrorist violence. With the death of Özal, the subsequent elevation of Demirel to the Presidency, and the retirement of İnönü, two relative neophytes to national politics, Tansu Ciller and Murat Karayalçin, assumed their respective party's leaderships and took over the DYP-SHP coalition government, but they, too, made little discernable progress in addressing the underlying social and economic inequalities they inherited from their predecessors.

What is clearly called for is a two-step process combining significant steps towards the lifting of all remaining bans (including broadcasting in Kurdish) still stifling Kurdish cultural expression, together with an effective drive to militarily put an end to Kurdish PKK terrorism. However, statements made by both President Demirel and Chief of Staff Doğan Güreş in 1993 point to a consensus in the ruling circles that no steps toward full right of expression for Turkey's Kurdish minority will be taken until the threat represented by the PKK is totally suppressed (Özkök, 1993). This policy has heretofore failed to solve the problem, although one can understand the government's rationale, that taking liberalizing steps could be claimed by the PKK as concessions to their movement.

Meanwhile, Turkish-Kurdish ethnic violence continues to spread away from southeast Anatolia and there have been severe clashes between Turks and Kurds in cities such as Antalya and Muğla. What this means is that partially and fully assimilated Kurds living far from their traditional homeland are having their ethnicity forced upon them by the actions of a Turkish majority growing increasingly apprehensive about the unrest spreading from the southeast. In short, this is a classic formula for a spiralling growth of the problem.

The Pan-Turkish / Pan-Ottomanism Taboo

The genius of Mustafa Kemal in nation-building was best demonstrated in the way he managed to shift the focus of Turkey's citizenry away from what was lost as a result of the Empire's collapse (no easy task given that a fair percentage of the 1920s population were actually refugees from one or another former Ottoman province), and concentrate it upon what was left. Specifically, the *misak-i milliye* (the National Pact) defined the territory of the new Turkish Republic. Turks were defined as those people living within the boundaries of this new state. Paradoxically, while they were claimed to be descendants of the Central Asian Turkish race, no attention was focused on either fellow Turkic ethnics in the Soviet Union, or on those Turks and Muslims left behind in Iraq and throughout the Balkans. In other words, the role of Turks in history was exaggerated while present-day Turks living outside the boundaries of Turkey were ignored. This attitude developed into a taboo against any kind of expression that could be viewed as Pan-Turanic or Pan-Ottoman in nature. Aside from the slight blip on the screen of Turkey's interests represented by Hatay, a problem solved by 1938–39, Turkish foreign policy in the first generation was status quo-ist and conservative, that is it was designed to protect the state's boundaries as defined in the *misak-i milliye*. In the same vein, Turkish military and strategic considerations were focused almost exclusively on the one neighbor who conceivable had the strength and even the desire to alter the status quo: the Soviet Union.

The outlook was defensive and protectionist, and it remained unchallenged throughout the Atatürk years and well into the 1950s. The first challenge to this policy developed in the mid-fifties over the treatment of the Turkish community in Cyprus. Interestingly, it was Turkish public opinion, stirred up considerably by the writing of one Hikmet Bil in the mass-circulation daily *Hürriyet,* that pulled the government into this particular quagmire. Likewise, it was largely in response to public opinion, aroused by Greek persecution of the Turkish minority, that in 1974 Prime Minister Bülent Ecevit opted to intervene militarily in the island republic. Today, over two decades later, Turkey has still not managed to untangle itself from Cyprus, nor does there appear to be any hope of it doing so in the immediate future. Interestingly, in Turkey's one unilateral military action beyond its own borders in the Republican era, it has become mired down and is seemingly unable to extricate itself from the Cyprus impasse. Yet despite this less than auspicious beginning to a more activist foreign policy, Turkey today stands at risk of being drawn into military conflicts in the Caucasus, with Iraq, and in the Balkans, should the Serbian "ethnic cleansing" move from Bosnia to Kossova and Macedonia. Granted, that in each of these instances Turkey is being drawn by forces outside its own complete control: the collapse of the Soviet Union and the nasty quarrel between the Caucasian Republics of Armenia and Azerbaijan over control of Nagorono Karabagh; the Gulf War with Saddam Hussein and Turkey's role as a member of the allied coalition; and the misguided dream of a greater Serbia propagated by the radical Serbian element in the population of the former Yugoslavia. But it is the willingness of Turkey's political leaders to project the country as a regional power, coupled with the changing neighborhood, that has resulted in a situation where the long-held taboo against concerning oneself with Turks/Muslims outside the country's borders has been discarded.

In each of the above-cited examples there is also a role played by ethnic groups in Turkey, who following the lifting of the ethnicity taboo are now organizing and speaking out on behalf of their fellow Bosnians, their fellow Azeris, or their fellow Kurds. In addition, the entire Turkish public is open to the resonance of this message. The ground is fertile. This is one more indication of the impact ethnic politics are making on the formulation of Turkey's foreign policy.

A case study of the situation in Bosnia during the early 1990s illustrates how this process occurs. Numerous Turkish print and television journalists reported from Sarajevo and their stories frequently covered the visits of a whole series of Turkish politicians to the area. Local organizations of Balkan Turks in the major cities in Turkey churned out daily press releases on the carnage as well. Many, if not most, of these reports condemned the western (read: Christian) world for not reacting in the Balkans in the same manner they did in Iraq when U.N. resolutions were violated. There were even calls in the Turkish press for some kind of military intervention on Turkey's part. So great was the pressure thus exerted on the government that the Turkish General Staff was (in a rare bit of candor) forced to go public explaining why military intervention was impossible, given the heretofore essentially defensive nature of Turkey's military preparedness. However, stories on Turkey's planned military acquisitions in the coming years include the news that the Turkish Air Force will be purchasing airborne refueling tankers, obviously with the intent of extending the country's military reach.

This Turkish drum-beating does not generate a very loud reaction from Turkey's traditional allies, its fellow NATO members, who are themselves searching for a new definition of their role in a world bereft of the Soviet Union and the Warsaw Pact. It is this vacuum, created by the collapse of Turkey's one-time singular focus on the eastern bloc, into which Turkey is being increasingly drawn.

Here, too, a leading role was until recently played by Turgut Özal, who, minus the real authority he became accustomed to as Prime Minister, still managed to shape a good deal of the discourse in Turkey from his largely ceremonial post as President. Talk of vaguely defined movements such as "Neo-Ottomanism" and a "Second Republic" emanated from sources close to the President, and shortly before his death he spurred the discussion by personally chairing a public debate that featured proponents of these concepts (journalist Cengiz Çandar and academic Nur Vergin [Güç *et al*, 1993: pp. 10–31]). What is meant by those using this terminology is difficult to fully comprehend. What is clear is the reaction such discussions generate from Turkey's immediate neighbors, all of whom suffer to varying degrees from phobias associated with anything resembling the rebirth of the Ottoman Empire. Here, too, the proponents of these theories in Turkey suffer from never having studied the nationalist histories of the former Ottoman peoples, and consequently somewhat blithely continue to press buttons without any apparent awareness of the responses that may result.

The eagerness with which certain groups in Turkey have sought to embrace their Turkic cousins in the former Soviet Union presents yet another example of how the failure to view oneself as seen by others can cause serious problems. Much of this type of rhetoric emanating from Turkey is far more reminiscent of views associated with Enver Paşa than with the thinking of Mustafa Kemal Atatürk. It reeks of the more extremist pan-Turanic/pan-Turkish rhetoric of the Young Turk period, and listening to it from present-day Turkey sends shivers up the spines of, among others, both Russians and Armenians. Attitudes until recently associated only with the most radical Turkish nationalist fringe, that of Colonel Alpaslan Türkeş and his followers, can now be heard frequently on radio and television. The ultimate dichotomy in this regard stems from the fact that Turkey is simply not able, economically or militarily, to effectively project its presence outside its borders. This does not however mean that Turkish voices cannot be heard and indeed listened to by all her neighbors, each of whose nationalistic histories are overfilled with Turcophobia.

What we have seen since the beginning of the nineties is a 180-degree reversal of Turkish foreign policy. A policy that at the outset was focused almost exclusively within the confines of its primary link to the west, the NATO Alliance, has veered off its traditional course. Today a multitude of voices are heard in the print and electronic media on behalf of Turks in Russia, Central Asia, the Caucasus, as well as Turkmens in Iraq, the Thracian Turks of Greece and Bulgaria, and even more alarmingly for the non-Turkish Muslim peoples of the former Yugoslavia and Albania. Though clearly these transformations result from changes in the political realities of the region, the swing has taken us from an almost total neglect of Turks and former Ottoman Muslim peoples into a situation in which a wide variety of peoples with only marginal relations to the Turks of Anatolia are clamoring for and receiving the ear of not only Ankara, but an ever-growing segment of the Turkish public as well.

Some of this euphoria may well be credited simply to the fact that for most of the past seventy years Turkey has stood alone as the only Turkish state in the world. This, coupled with a less-than-successful economic position, meant that Turkish politicians, when they had contact with the heads of other governments, generally did so in the role of supplicant.

Suddenly, the roles are reversed, and now a steady stream of heads of state flows in and out of Ankara seeking this or that support from Turkey. While this may well gratify the egos of the officials thus solicited, in real terms it simply diverts time and energy from an ever-mounting cycle of domestic problems.

One thing is certain: the taboo against involvement in regional problems outside the boundaries of the *misak-i milliye* has been broken by a combination of external and internal factors to which the country is quickly adapting. What is less certain is if and when a meaningful new *Weltanschauung* is going to emerge to replace that now discarded. While newspapers occasionally carry stories suggesting a reorganization in the Ministry of Foreign Affairs, one which would upgrade the role of policy planning, in reality, Turkish foreign policy in the early 1990s (not unlike that of many other nations in today's rapidly changing world) has consisted primarily of short-term "crisis-management" or "fire-fighting" efforts. The taboo is broken, the old order has clearly collapsed. In Turkey, as in many other countries, it is still too early to determine what will replace it.

The Information Taboo

No discussion of taboo-breaking in Turkey would be complete were it to ignore the sweeping transformations that have affected both the Turkish print and electronic media in the past five years.

While print press freedom has been an on-and-off proposition in Turkey throughout the past seventy years, the role of the press has always been important as a buttress to the state. In the past thirty years, military interventions in 1960, 1971, and 1980 were followed by retroactive prosecution of journalists for stories they had filed in the years leading up to the interventions. This fact may well have had some restraining effect upon journalists even in the best of times. In addition, laws prohibiting any defamation of Atatürk or the President also served to limit expression. However, it was through its role as the exclusive source of newsprint and all state-financed newspaper advertising that the government traditionally exercised a restraining hand on journalism.

This fact, coupled with a governmental monopoly on the electronic media (until the late eighties both radio and television news closely resembled that found in the eastern bloc), gave a distinct advantage to the party in power—be it elected or there as a result of a military coup. Officially, this taboo on the electronic media still exists. In fact, however, an ever-growing number of entrepreneurs, inspired no doubt by the Özallian version of a free-market economy, have managed to subvert the regulation by beaming first television and then radio signals into Turkey via satellite from outside the country, although most of the programming is actually done in Turkey. In turn, private radio and television stations have become one of Turkey's fastest growing industries. At last count there were over a dozen such private television channels and close to two hundred radio stations either in operation or in the planning stages. Given this plethora of forums, the average viewer, depending on his or her inclination, can watch the gamut of programming from pornography (which is reportedly particularly popular in Konya), to Islamic and to pan-Turanic. The government is still trying to come up with some means of regulating these endeavors, but to date there has been no success. The impact of this sudden electronic media growth is paralleled in the print area as well. Here, dozens of new weekly magazines are vying for the reader's attention.

While viewable as simply a natural part of the consumer oriented society that Turkey's free-market economy has spawned for that portion of the population able to afford the products whose advertising pays for both the print and electronic media explosion, these changes also need to be evaluated in light of our primary concern, namely, their contribution to the further breakdown of taboos in Turkey. Here they have a dual role: on the one hand this phenomenon itself represents the breaking of the taboo under which the flow of information was controlled in Turkey for most of the past seventy years; on the other hand, the new outlets for expression are providing the means by which the previously discussed taboos on history, religion, ethnicity, and pan-Turkism are broken.

One result of these changes is that for perhaps the first time in its history the Republic of Turkey truly has a free press. Indeed, on occasion, the media comes close to crossing the line between press freedom and press anarchy. The barriers to free expression in Turkey have clearly fallen: what is less certain is where this new found freedom will lead.

The Ultimate Taboo: Atatürkçülük

The legacy of the Republic's founding father, Mustafa Kemal Atatürk, has been closely guarded, used and misused, and frequently cited by practically every politician since the death of Atatürk on November 10, 1938. Sometimes associated with the "six arrows" of the RPP, in a wider sense it may be defined as a unique nationalist political ideology, or the ideological foundation of the Turkish Republic.

While all have claimed it, none have guarded it so jealously as the Turkish military, who have three times overthrown democratically elected politicians whom they viewed as having strayed from the tenets of *Atatürkçülük*. For these guardians, it has always been an illegal, immoral, and unethical act to question any of its tenets. Yet, as our earlier discussion disclosed, it was the high command of the military itself that, following their intervention of September 12, 1980, contributed to the successful undermining of the tenet of secularism by instituting mandatory religious education in the theretofore laic school system.

In addition, the breaking of each of the other taboos discussed in this paper has likewise led to a continual erosion of *Atatürkçülük* throughout the past decade. Indeed, I would argue that the arrows of *Devletçilik*, or statism/étatisme, *Laiklik* (laicism), and the traditional meaning of *Milliyetçilik* (Turkish nationalism) have been more or less undermined by the breaking of the taboos discussed herein, together with the replacement of the statist economic system by the Özallian free-market reforms of the 1980s. Also, as noted earlier, it was with the removal of the taboos designed to protect these aspects of *Atatürkçülük* that a fourth arrow, that of *Halkçılık*, popular sovereignty or democracy, began to be more fully manifested in Turkey.

Although *Atatürkçülük* developed more as the creation of Mustafa Kemal's successors, rather than a formal policy laid down by Atatürk himself, any questioning of its tenets, as interpreted by each new generation's leaders, was the ultimate taboo, the breaking of which was almost certain to bring down the wrath of the *devlet* on the transgressor. Today, more than fifty years after the death of Atatürk, and following over a decade of radical economic and social changes in the Republic he founded, not only his legacy is challenged on all fronts, but in many areas its impact continues to be steadily eroded.

* * * * * * * * * * * * * * *

Turkey today is a nation of over sixty million people, two thirds of whom are under twenty-five years of age, while close to half the population are under sixteen years old (DEİK, 1991: p. 28). Not only does this runaway population growth place inordinate strains on the existing educational infrastructure, it also means that the collective memory of at least 40 million Turks is relatively brief. Most cannot remember a Turkey in which Turgut Özal was not either Prime Minister or President. The majority cannot fully remember the details of the terrorist violence of the late 1970s that precipitated the military intervention of 1980. Those who can actually recall the first Prime Ministership of Süleyman Demirel in 1965 are a rapidly shrinking minority.

For earlier generations who have lived in the republic, the speeches and phrases they memorized provided a kind of intellectual underpinning, a common vocabulary that shaped their identities as citizens of Turkey. For the majority of Turks alive today, who came of age in the 1980s, Mustafa Kemal's legacy is that of a historical figure, one whose speeches they are forced to memorize in school, not the all-seeing, all-wise father figure that their parents came of age learning to revere.

If, as this paper has repeatedly implied, the lifting of the taboos which served to protect the Atatürk legacy has resulted in a weakening of the cement holding the country together, the real question must be what is going to replace the Kemalist ideology in the coming generation. For, faced with a rapidly changing world, the Ataturkist taboos on religion in politics, ethnic divisiveness, and the lure of pan-Turanism all increasingly appear as testimony to his statesmanship. He built a nation-state out of the remains of a crumbling empire and he did so without the kind of ethnic bloodletting going on in Bosnia, without the fanatic retrogression of Islamic Iran, and without the ethnic conflict threatening to dismember what is left of the former Soviet Union.

The present generation of Turkey's leaders appears to be fully engrossed in the day-to-day running of the country, seemingly unaware of the fact that a free-for-all free-market economy is not a substitute for a solidifying ideology. Likewise, Turkish intellectuals as a whole have generally failed to address the issue of a new definition of Turkey, or to offer explanations to account for the collapse of an ideology which has held the state together for seven decades.

There are the occasional voices speaking of a vaguely defined *İkinci Cumhuriyet*, among them that of the late President Özal. But what such a "Second Republic" means is unclear. The traumatic changes Turkey has undergone in the past decade are comparable only in scope and magnitude to those that replaced the Ottoman Empire with the First Republic. That they are occurring in the minds and attitudes of the Turkish public make their impact no less important than the drastic changes instituted by law in the early years of the Republic. To many, raised under the leader-cult of Atatürk and İnönü, what is lacking today is a single figure who can grasp and give voice to these changes in the way that Mustafa Kemal Atatürk did in the 1920s and 1930s. To others, the missing element may be political parties that represent a broader aggregate of political and social interests. For Turkish political parties in general (the only exception being the Motherland Party at the time of its creation in 1983) fail to reach out to a broad representative base of support which would allow them to build a consensus. Instead, by focusing on one segment of society, they lead to continual fragmentation. While the 1982 Constitution contains specific clauses designed to thwart this tendency, a decade later there are eight different political party groups represented in the Parliament (Sayari, 1993).

Without the emergence of some dialogue and consensus to guide it through the stormy waters of the "New World Disorder," Turkey's future is unclear. Failure to develop such consensus raises the all too real possibility that the country could slip into the kind of ethnic and religious chaos spreading like a virus throughout the region. In short, the challenge of Turkish democracy in the 1990s is to redefine its course taking into account its multi-ethnic character, the religious faith of a growing number of its inhabitants, and the growing economic inequality between the small minority of haves and the rapidly growing majority of have nots. The taboos that once limited democratic expression, while simultaneously serving to buttress the state elite ideology, have been erased; the question is: what will replace them?

Bibliography

DEİK, 1991: Dış Ekonomik İlişkiler Kurulu (Foreign Economic Relations Board), *Turkey, 1991:An International Comparison.* İstanbul (DEİK), p. 118.

Ersanel, 1993: Nedret Eransel, "'Değişen Türkiye 'de Siyaset' Paneli: Başka Türkiye Yok," *Nokta* (24–30 January), pp. 24–26.

Fuller, 1992: Graham E. Fuller, *Turkey Faces East: New Orientations Towards the Mid-East and the Old Soviet Union.* A Rand Note (R-4232-AF/A). Santa Monica, California (RAND), ix, 65 p.

Güç *et al*, 1993: Mehmet Güç, Can Karakaş, & Kudret Yahyaoğlu, "Uğur Mumcu Dosyası: Türkiye Bile Bile, Bilinmeyeni Yaşıyor," *Nokta* (January 31–February 6), pp. 10–31.

Henze, 1992: Paul Henze, *Turkey: Toward the Twenty First Century.* A Rand Note (N-3558-AF/A). Santa Monica, California (Rand), ix, 42 p.

Hughes, 1992: Lyttle Preston Hughes, *Atatürk, Atatürkçülük and Political Development in Turkey.* (Unpublished Ph.D. Dissertation, University of Mississippi), x, 259 p.

Kahveci, 1987: Adnan Kahveci, "On the Question of Ethnic Problems in Turkey," *Turkish Daily News*, Tuesday, June 2, p. 2.

Lesser, 1992: Ian O. Lesser, *Bridge or Barrier?: Turkey and the West After the Cold War.* A Rand Note (R-4204-AF/A). Santa Monica, California (Rand), ix, 47 p.

Lewis, 1992: Bernard Lewis, "Why Turkey?" (Unpublished paper presented at the Princeton University Late Ottoman Seminar, October 15), p. 17.

Ozel, 1993: Soli Ozel, "Neo Osmanlı Sevdasına İhtar!" *Nokta* (January 17–23), p. 74.

Özkök, 1993: Ertuğrul Özkök, "PKK, Bu Yaz Halledilecek," *Hürriyet*, January 16.

PIAR, 1/13/1993: PIAR Gallup Poll, *Turks Continue to View U.S. Unfavorably.* United States Information Agency (Opinion Research Memorandum: January 13), Washington, D.C., p. 8.

PIAR, 1/29/1993: PIAR Gallup Poll, *Turks Prefer Close Ties With Central Asia or Western Europe over Middle East or U.S.* United States Information Agency (Opinion Research Memorandum: January 29), Washington, D.C., p. 11.

Sayari, 1993: Sabri Sayari, *The New Leadership Generation in Turkey.* U.S. Department of State: Bureau of Intelligence and Research/ Office of Research. Washington, D.C., p. 63.

Sayari, 1992: Sabri Sayari, "Turkey: The Changing European Security Environment and the Gulf Crisis," *Middle East Journal*, vol. 46, no. 1 (Winter), pp. 9–21.

A Feminist Mirror in Turkey: Portraits of Two Activists in the 1980s

YEŞIM ARAT

But what can we do if we don't resemble democracy, we don't resemble socialism, we don't resemble anything? Gentlemen, we should be proud of defying comparison! Because, gentlemen, we resemble ourselves! (Kemal Atatürk, from a speech delivered on December 1, 1921)[1]

We were both surprised, when I so earnestly agreed with the friend who brought out a pack of cards and showed with pride the 'shaik' he had drawn to replace the king and the 'janissary' he had drawn to replace the jack and who argued for the necessity of distributing these cards in the two and a half million tables of the hundred and seventy thousand coffee shops of our country. (The protagonist of Orhan Pamuk's Yeni Hayat describing his encounter with a fervent nationalist in a coffee shop of a remote Anatolian town.)[2]

Partha Chatterjee argues that the global process of nation-building was transformed into an indigenous experience for the postcolonial world through the realm of culture (Chatterjee, 1993). The indigenous elites of the newly founded nation-states who adopted the political institutions of their Western colonizers could assert their autonomy as they underlined their cultural differences from their colonizers. They could "imagine" their new states not when they borrowed the Western socioeconomic and political institutions in the context of a universalizing modernization process, but when they articulated and elaborated their differences in values and norms to distinguish themselves from the West they had to imitate otherwise.

Chatterjee's argument provides insight into the Turkish experience as well. Founding fathers who instituted the Republic adopted Western political institutions and aimed to maintain the cultural specificity of the Turkish nation-state as they rewrote Turkish traditions, myths and history. Unlike many other developing countries, they rejected neither the West's institutions nor its values. Yet, they did resort to invented myths of Turkish traditions to justify adopting those Western norms. To borrow Orhan Pamuk's graphic description, while they were ready to play the card game imported from the West, they also changed the picture of the king and replaced it with the picture of a shaik and the jack with a janissary. Now the card game had indigenous colors. This was neither imitation nor provincialism. Turks would "resemble themselves" as they like to quote.

Women played a critical role in this venture. The Republican elite initiated Westernizing reforms, such as the 1926 Civil Code and the 1934 extension of suffrage to women, which had direct implications for women's status in society. Yet, while women were given rights to make them equal to men as in certain Western contexts,[3] they were also encouraged to play traditional domestic roles, meet prevailing notions of propriety for women, and behave like men in the public realm.[4] The cultural specificity of state feminism in Turkey was explicitly manifest in the institutional, cultural, and patriarchal control over women's sexuality. Women's sexuality could only be expressed through a culturally prescribed puritanic mode of behavior.

State feminism evolved and the unique role women played in the construction of the new Republic changed over time.[5] By the 1980s, Turkey had reached a different stage in the life of its Republic, in its socioeconomic and political development and in its relations with the West.[6] It was no longer taboo to criticize the Republican reforms; they were no longer idolized uncritically. In this context, women were active not merely as citizens of the new Republic, but as feminist critics of the state. They challenged state feminism as they engaged in redefining women's identities and their relation to the state.

Today, feminists in the West as well as critics in Turkey continue to inquire about the specificity of feminism in Turkey. There is concern among feminists in the West about Western cultural imperialism. Feminist scholars reflect on and are ready to hear indigenous feminist voices and criticisms.[7] They are interested in hearing the particular and the local stories lest the universalizing patterns of feminism in the West stifle the feminisms of their non-Western sisters.

Local critics share similar concerns about Western cultural imperialism but with different political motives. The underlying assumption common to critics with different political orientations is that feminism in Turkey is merely imitative. Both the liberals and the conservatives (e.g. the Islamists) advance arguments about the need for cultural authenticity and how feminists lack these concerns. The threat of cultural imperialism is used at times pejoratively, at times with a vengeance.

This paper argues that feminism in Turkey in the 1980s can be located in this unique process of change over at least two generations of feminists. The process attests to the peculiar transformation Turkey underwent in its politics and culture as well as its relations with the West. In contemporary Turkish politics, we can differentiate at least two different groups of feminists who, crudely speaking, belonged to different age groups. The first are the egalitarian Kemalist feminists who emphasize equal rights to men and for whom amendment of the Civil Code is a priority. The other are the more radical critics of the egalitarian feminists who emphasize women's personal liberation. The campaign against domestic violence was a highlight in this group's political activism (Tekeli, 1990; Sirman, 1989; Y. Arat, 1994). The tension, collaboration and animosity between egalitarian feminists and their more radical critics have set the parameters of the feminist scene in the 1980s.

This paper will focus on two prominent feminists of these two different generations and will be largely based on interviews conducted in the context of a project on the feminist movement in Turkey. We shall first study an egalitarian feminist as a prototypical example of the Kemalist feminists. Then we shall turn to a leading feminist critic who belongs to the younger generation of feminist forerunners of the 1980s. The interviews with these two important feminist activists took place in the spring of 1993 in their homes.

Karen Offen, in her work on the historical understandings and definitions of the term feminism, has shown the limitations of conceptualizing feminists as those who prioritize equal rights to men versus those who uphold sexual difference (Offen, 1992). She has convincingly argued that these conceptualizations dismiss the complexity of historically specific feminist identities; instead, she has characterized the alternate modes of feminist inclinations as "relational" rather than "individualist." Where "relational" feminism emphasizes women's rights as women in the context of a non-hierarchic male-female relationship, "individualist" feminism focuses on individual human rights regardless of gender (Offen, 1992, p. 76). In the Turkish case, Offen's criticisms of categorizing feminists as egalitarian (as opposed to difference feminists which we avoid discussing in this paper) are pertinent. The so-called egalitarian feminists seek more than merely equal rights to men; more significantly, the types of issues they have raised as "egalitarian" feminists have evolved over the mid-1980s and early 1990s. With due regard for Offen's criticisms, in this paper we shall use the term "egalitarian feminist" because this is how (some) feminists refer to themselves to differentiate the nature of their feminist inclinations from others, including those who identify themselves as radical feminists. In short, to explore the differences between different generations and kinds of feminists we will begin with their self-perceptions and descriptions.

Kemalist/Egalitarian Feminists

One of the four most active and visible advocates of egalitarian feminism in Turkey was a prominent doctor, publicly visible and recognized for her professional activism. She was born in 1935, twelve years after the proclamation of the Republic in 1923, nine years after the new civic code replaced the Shariat, and a year after suffrage was granted to women. A. K. had three younger brothers and a younger sister. Her father was an engineer and her mother, an educated Swiss expatriate, was an authoritative, disciplined homemaker. The oldest child of the family, A. K. reminisced on her childhood as follows:

> I lived during times when boys were regarded as more important than girls. For example, all my three brothers were sent to Galatasaray to be educated whereas I was sent to the local school.[8] My teachers enrolled me to kolej because I was a promising student. My father was livid with anger: how could that be . . . there was the Kandilli high school nearby. All the roads and the streets [on the way to kolej] which were full of dangers for a young girl going to school[9]. . . There is also the issue of protection, protection because you are a girl, not merely a lower regard [for girls]. In school there was an incidence of alopecia and our hair was cut. By mistake, someone called me young man. I had felt so happy. I had wished I was born a boy. We recognized the superiority of men in young age. Probably there was the desire to be a more authoritative person.

A. K. was keenly aware of her inferior standing in relation to boys both in her family and the society at large. Part of what constituted this lower standing was the alleged need for protection because of either inferiority, weakness, or lack of autonomy to protect oneself. This "need for protection" prevented her from attending an American high school that could have initiated her into a different world. As a person who wanted authority, she unabashedly desired to be like men. Later in life, after the younger generation of feminists became visible in the mid-1980s, she chose to call herself an egalitarian feminist. Her feminist activism predominantly centered on issues concerning women's equality to men, the amendment of the Civil Code and women's education.

An important aspect of this aspiration to be like men was an aspiration to be independent. Even though she had no ambition for riches, A. K. knew that practicing her profession paid for her autonomy. Two months after she began to be paid as a doctor and gained her economic independence, she divorced her husband, whom she had married when she was in medical school.

A. K.'s egalitarian feminism, with its emphasis on women's equality to men in economic, political, and social contexts, and the feminism of others who identify themselves as such, was nurtured on Turkish soil. Despite its universal resonances with basic tenets of human rights, egalitarian feminism, in the historically specific context of the 1980s' feminism in Turkey, was linked with Kemalist ideology, specifically, Kemalist nationalism, populism, and secularism. Aspirations for universal norms such as the equality that Republican populism entailed,[10] or rights to national sovereignty, were most explicitly articulated by Kemalist ideology when universal aspirations within an Islamic framework were rejected in favor of those within a Westernizing framework. To explore the links between egalitarian feminism in Turkey and Kemalism, we shall first discuss A. K.'s Kemalism and then trace its implications for her feminism.

A. K., like other egalitarian feminists (or at least the most visible public proponents of egalitarian feminism), was a woman of the so-called Kemalist generation. It was women like her and her parents that Kemalism had most directly influenced and who, in turn, had upheld the Kemalist flag. A. K. proudly claimed that she was an Ataturkist (Atatürkçü) and that she could not conceive of an alternative lifestyle. She thought that "we have all endorsed it like air and water." This explicit statement of Kemalism had ramifications.

If Kemalism adopted Turkish nationalism as a principle of political unity, A. K. grew up in this milieu. In her own words, "the children in the family were raised as Turks to the utmost." This socialization is all the more striking because A. K.'s mother was of Swiss origin. A. K. explains as follows:

> My mother was prohibited from speaking any other language. You are going to learn Turkish from the helper in the house and you are going to speak Turkish. Harsh times, in other words. When we were ten, they said to my mother, "Now, teach her English" and we learned English. We lived through such deformities, that is, the nationalism of those times. But of course it has nurtured very positive things in me. I am utmost committed to my country. I could never think, in a different country, that this country could be my

country. I lived in such an environment. Of course, when we interpret it later, I believe that great injustice was done to my mother. I would never tolerate such an injustice and I could not think of such an injustice done to others. They bring my mother and make her Muslim and all . . . .

A. K. is aware of the price her mother had to pay for the nationalist feelings the children were socialized into and which did provide an anchor and a source of pride for A. K. She is proud of her national loyalties despite her recognition of the exclusionary, repressive, and chauvinistic nature of the nationalism prevailing in her family.

A. K.'s nationalism also permeates into and defines her understanding of democracy. This conceptualization of democracy has clear implications for her stance on women's autonomy and choice. At the end of our discussion when she was asked if she had anything else to add, A. K. wanted to clarify her posture against contemporary criticisms levied against Kemalism which she said she had heard from some feminists as well. She argued that these people trace the advent of democracy in Turkey not to the proclamation of the Republic, but rather to the reversal of the policy in 1950 that thenceforth allowed the call to prayer to be read in Arabic, rather than in Turkish as had been the law after the foundation of the Republic. She said that "all of a sudden, in her own country, in a country where Turkish was spoken, no one had the right to do this" and explained that she was extremely opposed to those who interpreted this as democracy and could not find any explanation of how it could be considered democratic. Turkish nationalism demarcated the boundaries of A. K.'s concept of democracy. Nationalism was a necessary if not sufficient condition of democracy. If democracy meant self-rule and involved equal opportunity for self-rule, those who accepted Turkish would be eligible for its practice. As we shall discuss later, parameters of self-rule set by this particular nationalist understanding would have implications for A. K.'s attitude toward Islamist women.

Kemalist nationalist discourse, and the concept of democracy demarcated within this discourse, also provided the context and the boundaries within which feminism and women's rights were located for A. K. She argued that the women's movement did not begin with the "Kemalist revolution"; however, she thought that women "found themselves" with the Republican reforms.[11] In her own words,

> [The Kemalists] looked with a fully egalitarian perspective to the issue [of women's status]. But there are the traditions and customs; it won't end all of a sudden. As a doctor, I am a concrete example. Had I not lived in the Republican period, I would not have been at this point. So many beautiful things have come to women: male-female equality. You don't have to have a fight in order to get something. It has come so beautifully. If we exist today, if we can all think and talk, we owe this to all that the Republican era has secured for us. We exist because our mothers were educated. We exist because our fathers were educated.

From this perspective, the structure in which women's rights, identities, and status have been located by the Kemalists is not challenged. The "fully egalitarian" perspective is deemed satisfactory. If women have "found themselves" with the Republic, the assumption is that there was a self, an identity that needed to be discovered and that was discovered. What is needed is not to challenge the framework within which women's issues and women's identities have been defined, but rather, to fight tradition and custom in pursuit of the goals defined within this framework. The "concrete" example of the success of Republican reforms for women, in A. K.'s view, is becoming professional, in her case, a doctor. Elsewhere, she does admit that she feels she has never been exploited as a woman. Not all women had the opportunities she had, so what is needed is to enlighten women and extend to them the opportunities that only some elite women could have had at the advent of the Republic.

At this point, the links between egalitarian feminism in Turkey, their strategies for empowering women and Republican populism need to be elaborated. Populism, an important principle of Kemalist ideology written into the Constitution in 1937, involved government by the people as well as for the people (Lewis, 1976, pp. 256–7, 465–67; Shaw, 1977, pp. 378–84). During the one-party era, the concept of the "government for the people" helped legitimize an authoritarian rule which could pass policies despite the people. The Kemalist rule practically operated on and owed the success of its reforms to the principle of government by the people despite the people.

The rhetoric of the egalitarian feminists who propose to operate within a Kemalist paradigm[12] reflects the desire to take action on behalf of women who do not have the privileges these elite women do. A. K. is a good example. Even though she thinks she has not been exploited in her life,[13] she feels an empathy with women who live through what she has avoided. Throughout her professional life, she has often personally tried to help women clients, students, nurses, and villagers.

Yet, she strongly thinks that the state needs to be involved in promoting equality between men and women. She is an ardent advocate of what she herself calls "state feminism." At least till conditions of equality are ensured, state feminism, she argues, is necessary and "the alternative is not even a possibility." Drawing on the example of textile factories in Turkey, she underlines the crucial role the state has played in Turkey's development. She points out that whoever is the top executive will admit that he or she has been trained at Sümerbank (the state textile industry). She elaborates that securing equality in education will be possible only through national education. Consequently, it will be the state that will maintain egalitarian laws and enforce them.

A. K., who expects the state to play an ultimately critical role in advocating male-female equality, has a unique democratic understanding of citizenship and a liberal conception of the state. That the state vested with the important responsibility of securing equality might well act irresponsibly or misuse its responsibility or authority in authoritarian acts is not a possibility that bothers A. K. She is not afraid of the state's abuse of its authority because she feels democratic citizens will actively participate in civic life and force the state to act in the manner they dictate. She is confident that what this active citizenship dictates will be democratic and egalitarian. Her words are revealing:

> I mean the state is not any different in essence from us. . . .
> Some see the state as an institution at the top that imposes
> things on them . . . . a military institution. It should not be like
> that. We have understood the state wrong. The state is people
> we elect working for us according to law. Who is going to

defend my right? Who is going to protect the Republic, democracy, women's rights? I select him or her and say, "go do this for me." I don't see her or him as superior to me. This is my perspective. We should impose this [understanding] on the state.

This liberal conception of the state where the state—or more precisely the government—exists to respond to the constituents' demands, interestingly, goes hand in hand with a defense of the Jacobean Republican state that has initiated reforms including those concerning women's rights. It is assumed that all the citizens of the state are active, democratic participants who share A. K.'s values, for example, on issues of male-female equality. What is contested is not the underlying ideology or shared truth but rather how it is implemented. However, even though egalitarian state policies have been critical in improving women's opportunities, they have done so usually through a state which claimed to know the best interests of the populace at times, in spite of any opposition to its policies and ideology.

The roots of this "liberal" understanding of citizenship in the Turkish context are, unlike in the West, not rooted in an ethic of individualism. A. K.'s egalitarian feminism is not necessary derived from or ultimately legitimated by a faith in or moral grounding in individual rights. She is skeptical of individualism. When she elaborates her defense of state feminism and the necessity to work along with men, she comments on individualism as follows:

If we could rid ourselves of that individualism. I wonder if we have the right to be individualist feminists? I mean let us be individualist but let us also be organizational (orgutsel). Only then can we reach our goals more quickly. Different things can be done [to promote feminist goals], but we should share these differences.

A. K. has respect for these individualist feminists. She says that at times she finds herself defending and explaining why these radical feminists are the way they are and why there are those "who hate men." She explains that she admires some of their campaigns such as the "Purple Needle Campaign" (where the more radical feminists organized to distribute needles with purple ribbons to protect women against sexual harassment by men) or the collective divorce of feminists in protest of the conservative government's attempts to strengthen the traditional family. Ultimately, however, she feels that women could unite with a common denominator more than the radical feminists were ever willing to do. In other words, collective efforts, solidarity, and unity are what she feels will eventually determine the success of feminist goals, and the possibility of potential conflict within these goals is not a serious consideration.

If the egalitarian feminists are interested in using the state as an instrument to promote male-female equality and believe that collective action by citizens will push the state to enforce the appropriate policies, how will those citizens, especially women who do not share secular feminist goals, be dealt with? As a secular Kemalist, A. K. has endorsed the tradition of state feminism in Turkey. She believes that religion, including Islam, should belong to the private realm. She took private lessons in Islam in her early years and considers herself to be a faithful believer. Yet, she is vehemently opposed to the Islamists in the public arena, whom she depicts as reactionary conservatives. She claims that in Imam Hatip schools (religious middle-level schools) they teach that the world is flat and that these institutions do not belong to the contemporary world. Secure as she is of her knowledge of who the Islamists are and what they stand for, she believes that women who cover their heads are exploited and used by Islamist men. She explains as follows:

> I do not believe it is her free choice [to cover her head]. I am angry at those who have captured her brains. The way they have put her forward like a flag without showing and offering her options and by manipulating some material interests, this has caused me grief.

Throughout the discussion she reiterates that she believes women do not choose to cover their heads by their own will. She feels secure in her convictions and in her generalizations. That it might be a "free choice" for some women to cover their heads—whether in protest, in search of authentic identities, or in accommodation to changing modern circumstances—does not convince her.

The New Generation of Feminists

In the early 1980s, before the old generation visibly began calling itself Kemalist or egalitarian feminists, a younger generation of newly professional women emerged into the public realm with what were then truly novel feminist identities. Daughters of the earlier generation of Kemalist women, they did not need to identify themselves as Kemalists. In fact they were critical of the Kemalist heritage. Aware of the opportunities Kemalist reforms opened for women, they nevertheless chose to focus on what Kemalists did not accomplish, what they lacked and what they missed.

This new generation of women began questioning their Kemalist upbringing with their initiation into leftist ideology and intellectual circles. Disappointed as they were with the Turkish left's attitude to their problems (Berktay, 1995), these women began discovering feminism, shaping feminist identities for themselves and attempting to use feminism as a tool for sociopolitical criticism. The emergence of their feminist identities was organically linked to their criticism of the Kemalist project as well as to their criticism of the left, which had evolved under the Kemalist canopy.

Our interview with P. T. was revealing of this sociopolitical change; it is reflected in her attempt to define her feminist identity. P. T. was born in 1944. This was one year before the Democratic Party, which would carry Turkey to a multiparty democracy, was founded. Her parents, especially her mother, were staunchly Kemalist parents. Her parents were high school philosophy teachers who had helped introduce the new Republican generation to the values and traditions of the West. Since she was an only child, she did not feel the competition with boys within her family. After she finished high school in Ankara, she was sent abroad to France; she moved on to Switzerland and studied Political Science, eventually to become an associate professor at Istanbul University. Her mother, who had financed her studies abroad, was proud to see her daughter advance in her academic career. In P. T.'s words, academic career was her mother's "myth." In 1983, despite her mother's firm opposition, she resigned from the university in protest of the Board of Higher Education founded to centralize and oversee, if not control, the university system during the military rule. Her initiation into feminism and her feminist activism began with her break in her professional career in academia. She called herself an independent feminist.

P. T. did not trace her feminist consciousness to Republican reforms. If anything it was her friends, colleagues, acquaintances, and circumstances that precipitated her initiation into feminism. Her interest in political participation and Marxism had already led her to write a book on the subject before she began identifying herself publicly as a feminist. She was asked to work on a project on women for a publishing company after she resigned from her position at the university, and it was as she worked on this project that she began carving her feminist identity. With a close circle of friends, she became part of a group that they later identified as a consciousness-raising group. Unlike A. K., she did not recall being jealous of boys or trying to have their authority because all along she had identified and allied with them. She keenly remembered her condescension for what she called "incapable" girls in her classes who could not identify with boys. She grew up feeling equal to boys. It was through these intense discussions and revelations in her all female circle of friends that she began to look more critically at this cultivated equality and began searching for more systemic causes of it.

Kemalism, which she and her circle of friends were taught had liberated people like them was criticized. She was against its statism, its populism that legitimized elitist policies for the people, at times despite the people and despite its secularism.

For P. T., the reforms of the Republic that were an inspiration for egalitarian feminists defined the parameters which the feminists had to surpass. She granted that the Republic was important and that the reforms had been a necessary, but clearly not sufficient, condition of women's liberation. She was careful to disassociate herself from the rather simplistic contemporary critics who called themselves the "second Republicans"[14] and traced the cause of 1980s' problems to the authoritarianism that they linked to the foundation of the Republic. Her own words on the issue are curse and forceful:

> Well, the Republic has done things it had to do. It has not done things it could do. Also, now, stories of "this was done, we accomplished this" prevented what could be done from

being done. It took us fifty years. I mean fifty years had to pass for us to break the Kemalist taboo and the rhetoric of "we were given equal rights because of Atatürk." No, we did not have these rights because of Atatürk. Atatürk had to give these rights to us.

P. T.'s verdict on Kemalism, namely that we should go beyond it, and that women were the subjects who deserved their rights rather than the objects who were granted rights, is also reflected in her verdict on Kemalist or egalitarian feminists. She believes that egalitarian feminism is very important. Yet, she sees egalitarianism as a stage, or rather, a necessary but not sufficient condition in women's liberation. She thinks that you cannot accomplish anything for women unless you have an egalitarian legislative framework. In the Turkish context, however, what she contests with egalitarian feminists is their "Kemalist," namely elitist, attitude to women: she argues that "for the people, despite the people" attitude of Kemalism is reflected in the Kemalist feminists' attempt to "save other women." Throughout the interview P. T. again and again argues that Kemalist feminists are "women who have been liberated" and are "content with what they have" and "want to liberate other women." "These women have been liberated by Atatürk," P. T. contends, and "they think that they do not have problems and that peasant women do and working class women do and the state has to address these." According to P. T., feminism begins by challenging this traditional relationship of elite women to other women, to themselves, and to the state. Questions need to be posed as to how far they themselves are liberated, if someone else can liberate another, and what the role of the state is in this "liberation" process.

The relationship of the younger generation of feminists to the state was different from that of the Kemalist egalitarian feminists. The contrast was vividly reflected in P. T.'s conception of the state in relation to A. K.'s. A. K.'s liberal state was far removed from P. T.'s authoritarian one. P. T. explained as follows:

> For one thing, the state is something above the society. And you as the citizen in this society, go and pay your taxes, go and suffer in its door all to uphold the state . . . . I basically see the state of the Turkish Republic this way. In other

words, the society exists for the state, the great Turkish state. However, the important thing is what happens in the society, what happens to real people. There are things that these real people can do for themselves, and I think at times the state even obstructs these.

Since P. T. is a political scientist aware of alternate conceptions of the state, her depiction of the authoritarian, alienating Turkish state is a conscious rendition of her personal experience, one clearly at odds with that of A. K. P. T. feels that the authoritarian state can be a liability rather than an asset for feminists. P.T. promptly criticizes the Minister of State responsible for women's affairs for promising to open a women's shelter in every province of the country. According to P. T., the promise which many egalitarian feminists would applaud is ill conceived because shelters should not be founded through central planning. First, small women's groups should put together the project, find the people to carry it out and then approach the government, preferably the local government, to help them out with the money and the site and the acquisition of the appropriate cadres. The centralizing, monolithic power of the state is seen as a threat to local feminist initiatives. P. T explains as follows:

> [The] state is a locus that irons out and minimizes differences in order to generalize. That is why it exists. It exists as a center to unite different interests. If it plunges in to assume these tasks, it means repression, detainment, prevention and obstruction of tasks which could be accomplished with real local initiatives.

At the core of P. T.'s criticism of Kemalist populism and state feminism is her radically different grounding in feminism. Unlike the egalitarian feminists who were inspired by the populist nationalist state feminism of the Republic, P. T.'s inspiration for feminism is ultimately individualistic. Her feminism begins with the individual, and its goal is an expansion of opportunities and choice for the individual. She believes that even the feminist movement is an "individualistic movement" and explains as follows:

> If we are here all together, we are here one by one as indi-

viduals. None of us is after being a leader, but we all want every one of us to be accepted as what we are. We are not for example the soldiers or the laymen of the revolutionary or anyone else. We did not accept this. If this is a criticism it is true. This is our weakness. Everyone wanted to develop as herself in her own rhythm . . . . No soldiers for the feminist revolution!

Even though P. T. traces women's oppression to power relations between men and women embedded in societal structures, her fulcrum or her anchor is the individual woman. It is for the individual woman's personal choice, including her rights to sexual liberation, that she wages her feminist fight.

This respect for individual choice is reflected in her attitude toward Islamist women as well. Unlike the Kemalist egalitarian feminists, P. T. is inclined to give the Islamist women who cover their heads the benefit of doubt, and bases her stance on their claims for individual choice. While she does see the societal causes of the Islamist covering, P. T. ultimately chooses to tolerate the headscarf because it is the Islamist woman's choice. In her words, "the women want to study, they want to reach for the better, they want to change their lives." She charges the Kemalist feminists with trying to prevent these women from being educated after they (the Kemalists) have insisted so hard on the significance of education for women. If, she argues, you look at the situation from a woman's perspective and if women are your point of departure, you cannot prevent these women from entering the university with covered heads.

Considerations on the Two Feminisms

Feminists and feminism in Turkey evolved as the society was transformed in the context of an increasingly smaller world. Mustafa Kemal, who in 1921 claimed that Turks resemble themselves, helped expand opportunities to women and initiated state feminism. In the long term, feminists in Turkey who "resembled themselves" helped reconstruct and redefine feminist identities that had been handed down to them. Like many feminists in the West, Kemalist feminists upheld egalitarian norms and sought male-female equality; yet they resembled themselves because their egalitarian feminism was shaped by Kemalist nationalism and its particular brand of "for the people despite the people" populism. Like A. K., Kemalist feminists seek equality within the confines of a secular nationalist ideology and with the help of an effective state. This is a framework where women's needs are already determined and there is no room for heterogeneity; in this framework, it is hard to reconcile the differing demands articulated by groups such as Islamist women and radical feminists.

Just as A. K. and her feminism mirror the world-view of the founding fathers of the Republic and portrays how Kemalist feminists resemble themselves, P. T. mirrors the changes that have taken place over time. Like many other feminists in the West, P. T. also believes that women should seek equality as well as difference. Yet, P. T., like other feminists of her generation in Turkey, molds her feminist identity by situating herself against the Kemalists and Kemalist feminists. The new generation wants to go beyond the male-female equality guaranteed by the state to accommodate women's differences, options, and choices, including those for sexual liberation. They are skeptical of a state that seeks to change things in the name of women, a trademark of Kemalist feminism. Unlike feminists in the West, the younger generation reconstructs its feminism in opposition to its Kemalist history and statist ideology. Ultimately, both the Kemalist feminists and the younger generation of critics are influenced by feminists in the West and work those feminist concepts out in the Turkish context. Their experience mirrors that of the Turkish society itself.

Feminist experience in the 1980s is not confined to the discourse between the Kemalist egalitarian feminists and their younger critics. The critics have been duly criticized by an even younger generation of women who do call themselves radical feminists. The proliferation of the debate which displays the expanding scope of feminist experience in Turkey attests to the vitality of social and political change in the country. Borders are perforated, influences from the West are refracted in response to problems articulated in the changing local context. The feminist spectrum in contemporary Turkish society mirrors the drive for a more open society that "resembles itself."

References

Abadan-Unat, Nermin, 1981, "Social Change and Turkish Women," in Nermin Abadan-Unat, ed., *Women in Turkish Society*, Leiden, E.J. Brill.

Altan, Mehmet, 1992, " 'İkinci Cumhuriyet' Nedir, Ne Değildir," *Bülten*, December, 1992.

Arat, Yeşim, 1994, "Toward a Democratic Society: The Women's Movement in Turkey in the 1980s," *Women's Studies International Forum*, vol. 17, no. 23.

Arat, Zehra, 1994, "Turkish Women and the Republican Reconstruction of Tradition," in Fatma Müge Göçek and Shiva Balaghi, eds., *Reconstructing Gender in the Middle East: Power, Identity and Tradition*, N.Y., Columbia University Press.

Berktay, Fatmagül, 1995, "Has Anything Changed in the Outlook of the Turkish Left on Women," in İ. Tekeli, ed., *Women in Modern Turkish Society*, London, Zed Books.

Chatterjee, Partha, 1993, *The Nation and Its Fragments*, Princeton, Princeton University Press.

Durakbaşa, Ayşe, 1988, "Cumhuriyet Döneminde Kemalist Kadın Kimliğinin Oluşumu," *Tarih ve Toplum*, March.

Göle, Nilüfer, 1991, *Modern Mahrem*, İstanbul, Metis Yayınları.

Heper, Metin, Ayşe Öncü, and Heinz Kramer, 1993, *Turkey and the West*, London, I.B. Tauris and Co.

Heper, Metin, 1992, " 'İkinci Cumhuriyet Tartışmaları' Üzerine," in *Bülten*, December.

Kandiyoti, Deniz, 1989, "Women and the Turkish State: Political Actors or Symbolic Pawns," in N. Yuval-Davis and F. Anthisas eds. *Women-Nation-State*, London, Macmillan.

Kili, Suna, 1994, "Modernleşme ve Kadın," in Necla Arat ed. *Türkiye'de Kadın Olmak*, İstanbul, Say Yayınları.

Lewis, Bernard, 1976, *The Emergence of Modern Turkey*, London, Oxford University Press (2nd edition, first issued in 1968).

Offen, Karen, 1992, "Defining feminism: a comparative historical approach," in Gisela Bock and Susan James, eds., *Beyond Equality and Difference*, London, Routledge.

Pulur, Hasan, 1995, "Biz bize benzeriz (2)," *Milliyet*, July 15, p. 3.

Shaw, Stanford J., and Ezel Kural Shaw, 1977, *History of the Ottoman Empire and Modern Turkey*, vol. 2, Cambridge, Cambridge University Press.

Signs: Journal of Women in Culture and Society, 1993, vol. 18, no. 4, Summer.

Sirman, Nükhet, 1989, "Feminism in Turkey: A Short History," *New Perspectives on Turkey*, vol. 3.

Tekeli, Şirin, 1990, "Women in the changing political Associations of the 1980s," in Andrew Finkel and Nükhet Sirman, eds., *Turkish State, Turkish Society*, London, Routledge.

Notes

I would like to acknowledge the Middle East Research Competition of, the Ford Foundation which made the research for this paper possible.

1. Lewis, 1976, p. 465. Lewis adds this comment in a footnote: "the last phrase has become a favourite text for quotation." The last phrase has indeed remained a favorite text for quotation since Lewis first published his book in 1961. The columnist Hasan Pulur argues that while Mustafa Kemal might have made this claim to defend the incipient Republic against its critics, the text is now often used as self-criticism (Pulur, 1995).

2. Orhan Pamuk, *Yeni hayat* (İstanbul: İletişim, 1994), 90; the passage was translated by Y. Arat.

3. Turkish people, including social scientists, have traditionally been very proud to underline that European countries like France, Italy, Belgium, Switzerland extended suffrage to women after 1934.

4. This paper does not examine the Republican reforms concerning women. For various interpretive views on the subject see Abadan-Unat, 1981; Kili, 1994; Kandiyoti, 1989; Tekeli, 1990; Nilüfer Göle, 1990; Ayşe Durakbaşa, 1988.

5. On the historical evolution of feminism in Turkey, see Sirman, 1989; on the emergence of feminism in the 1980s, see Tekeli, 1990; on the significance of feminist activism for democratic politics, see Arat, 1994.

6. On the perception of the West by different groups in Turkey and its implications for changing political values and identity, see Heper et al., 1993.

7. See the call for papers that address postcolonial, emergent, and indigenous feminisms for the special issue of *Signs: Journal of Women in Culture and Society* (Summer 1995), in *Signs*, Summer 1993, p. 989.

8. Galatasary is the prestigious French lycee where the language of instruction was French, whereas *kolej* is the American High School for Girls, in this case the one located at Üsküdar. On the historical context and import of these schools for the Turkish cultural context, see Lewis, 1976, p. 122.

9. Material in brackets was added to clarify the context and substance of what was transmitted in the interview.

10. On Kemalist populism see Lewis, 1976, pp. 256–57, 465, 467 and Shaw, 1977, pp. 378–84.

11. A. K. uses the word "revolution" in referring to Republican reforms (*Cumhuriyet devrimleri* in Turkish), which reveals her assessment of the impact of the reforms.

12. By Kemalist paradigm, I mean the framework in which rights and responsibilities of and expectations from women were defined by the Kemalist founding fathers.

13. She has said this twice during the interview without being questioned or probed on this issue. Apparently, she is interested in divorcing her commitment to feminism from her personal experience of exploitation.

14. On this debate, see the special issue of *Bülten*, December 1992, for example the articles by Mehmet Altan, "İkinci Cumhuriyet Nedir, Ne Değildir?" (What Is the Second Republic and What It Is Not?) and Metin Heper, "İkinci Cumhuriyet Tartışmaları Üzerine" (On the Second Republic Debate), pp. 2–7 and 8–13.

JOURNAL OF WORLD HISTORY

Devoted to historical analysis from a global point of view, featuring comparative and cross-cultural scholarship and research on processes that work their influences across the boundaries of cultures and civilizations.

• ARTICLES OF NOTE •

Individual subscriptions (2 issues/year) are US$25/year and include membership in the World History Association (students, US$15/year with copy of valid ID). **INDIVIDUALS:** send address and checks (payable to World History Association) to Prof. Richard Rosen, World History Association, Department of History and Politics, Drexel University, Philadelphia, PA 19104, USA. **INSTITUTIONS:** send inquiries to University of Hawai'i Press, Journals Department, 2840 Kolowalu St., Honolulu, HI 96822, USA. Phone: (808) 956-8833. **ON THE WWW**— http://www2.hawaii.edu/uhpress/Journals/JW/JWHome.html